Additional Praise

"*The Long View* poses big questions about where our careers are going, and offers fresh answers. A global CEO provides valuable lessons and practical day-to-day exercises to help us get the most out of every stage of our careers."

> —Adam Grant, Wharton professor and *New York Times* bestselling author of *Originals* and *Give And Take*

"We are educated for a world that does not exist. This book provides one of the clearest, and most insightful roadmaps for inventing your career and life."

> —Peter Sims, author of *Small Bets* and Founder-CEO of Parliament, Inc.

"In this age of short-termism, this is a breath of fresh air. If you care about your career, *The Long View* is required reading, whether you are starting out or a seasoned executive. Full of practical advice and transcendent clarity, Brian provides answers to many of the workforce's biggest questions."

> —Don Tapscott, bestselling author of *Wikinomics* and *Blockchain Revolution*

"*The Long View* is an outstanding book which provides excellent advice for today's world of careers, which are different from even five years ago."

> —Dr. Karl Moore, faculty member at McGill University, bestselling author and columnist for *Forbes* and *The Globe & Mail*

"*The Long View* is a must read book, whether you're contemplating retirement or just starting out in your career. This is the first book that gives you a coherent plan for making the most of every stage in your career."

> —Dr. Chris Yeh, co-author of *New York Times* bestseller *The Alliance*

THE LONG VIEW

Career Strategies to Start Strong,

Reach High, and Go Far

Brian Fetherstonhaugh

JBFetherstonhaugh

DIVERSIONBOOKS

Diversion Books
A Division of Diversion Publishing Corp.
443 Park Avenue South, Suite 1008
New York, New York 10016
www.DiversionBooks.com

For more information, email info@diversionbooks.com

First Diversion Books edition September 2016.
Paperback ISBN: 978-1-68230-293-4
eBook ISBN: 978-1-68230-292-7

The Long View is dedicated to my wife, Chris,
and my daughters, Claire and Alison.
You inspire me every single day.

Contents

2   TACTICS THROUGH THE STAGES   97

3 CAREERS AND REAL LIFE 171

INTRODUCTION

The Career Revolution

Jennifer, Mark, and Emily are all going to work today. Despite their many differences, they do have one thing in common: they're all worried about their careers.

For twenty-two-year-old Jennifer, worry is mixed with anticipation. This is day one of her career. "I am so excited but so freaked," she says. "I've spent fifteen years getting educated, and today it's real. I can't ask my parents for advice. They have no clue what the job market is like today. Will I fit in? Will I ever find the perfect job? Will I have to jump around to get ahead?"

At forty-two, Mark feels like he's reaching the peak of his career. "I've paid my dues and built some skills. What's next? Can I do a bigger job without working longer hours and wrecking my family life?"

Emily is also asking some tough questions. With her fifty-fifth birthday right around the corner, she is contemplating retiring from her big corporate job. "I've sweated for over thirty years. So many of the people I grew up with are no longer here. I don't have enough money to totally retire from work, but there's no way I am going back into the big corporate world. If that's not it, then what's next? I get bored too easily. Bridge and golf just aren't going to cut it."

Jennifer, Mark and Emily are not alone. According to The Futures Company's 2015 Global Monitor survey of over 15,000 respondents in 23 countries, people in the workforce everywhere are feeling the heat. Globally, 58 percent feel strongly pressured to have a good job and career, rising to 64 percent among those 21–35 years old. Across all age groups, 53 percent feel pressure to acquire new skills and improve themselves. And among the Millennial generation (approximately ages 21–35), "becoming a successful entrepreneur" is behind only "having a long and successful marriage" on their list of top-ranked life goals.[1]

The idea of what a successful career looks like is changing fast, and many people are struggling to adapt to a host of new challenges. Millennials are seeing the decline of job security. They are taught to think about "The Brand of Me," but often lack the foundational skills and building blocks to succeed in the long haul. Mid-career professionals are feeling vulnerable as their jobs, industries, and entire careers face serious disruption. Those approaching traditional "retirement day" are finding themselves both healthier and poorer than ever before. What comes next? For much of our lives, we spend more time working than sleeping. Many of us spend more time wedded to our careers than to our

---

1   The Futures Company Global Monitor, 2015.

spouses. Some of us could easily spend 100,000 hours of our lives at work. And when we are not doing the work, we are often worrying about it. Worrying is not going to help. Instead, let's focus our energies on understanding how these big changes are creating a new set of tools, skills, and decisions that can help people at every stage of their careers. This book is about empowering you to take action to thrive in this new landscape.

The career revolution is upon us. Employer-employee loyalty is eroding. Retirement is starting later but lasting longer. A whole new wave of career choices is emerging—including job titles we've never seen before in industries we've never heard of. The corporate nine-to-five job has been replaced with a dizzying array of part-time, contract, job-sharing, remote, and entrepreneurial options. Career-minded people everywhere are seeking more flexibility and compatibility between their jobs and their personal lives. Job competition is coming from new quarters: from abroad, from younger people, from older people. And, increasingly, from machines.

Are you ready for the career revolution? Most people are not. We seem to have a few contradictory ideas about the nature of work. According to The Futures Company research, over 70 percent of people in the US agree with the statement "my future career will be decided based on what makes me happy rather than how much money I make." But in that same research, working people revealed that the number one factor in choosing where to work is money (86 percent agree), followed by benefits (82 percent agree).[2] Our aspirations of pursuing the work that will maximize our happiness are clashing with global economic instability. We want to dream but we're afraid. The world that we know is changing—fast.

We need new ways of finding jobs, and new ways to build careers that last. We need a new mind-set and a new tool kit. Not just tactics—but robust, road-tested strategies that will equip us to survive and thrive in the new career reality. The answer isn't to throw away everything we've known, but to choose the relevant bits, give them fresh context, and combine old-school wisdom with new-school context.

I have been mentoring and teaching on the subject of career development for over two decades. It began with an internal training speech twenty years ago to my employees at Ogilvy & Mather Canada, where I was president. I did it as a bit of a lark—just to give people a change of pace from their usual company training sessions—but I was surprised by the enthusiastic response. About ten years ago, I began lecturing at top business schools such as Yale, Columbia, NYU, McGill, and MIT Sloan. I always gave about half the lecture on my area of expertise—global marketing— and devoted the other half to sharing my thoughts on career management. In every single case, it was the career management advice that got the biggest reaction.

For the past decade, my day job has been as CEO of a 5,000-person global marketing company called OgilvyOne Worldwide. It is the digital marketing arm of Ogilvy & Mather, one of the world's leading advertising firms. It is a

---

2   The Futures Company USA, 2015. n = 1,644.

fantastic gig that comes with a very full schedule, including about 120 days of international travel every year. I started noticing that in addition to my day job, my calendar was being populated with a growing number of informal career consultations. Pretty much every week I shared breakfast, lunch, coffee, or dinner with some extremely bright and talented person seeking advice on careers. The more people I spoke with, the more I realized that I was giving out the same advice—the circumstances were all different, but the core of the challenges remained the same.

In early 2014, a colleague of mine suggested that I finally write down my long-simmering thoughts on career management. I had tons of material, gleaned from over twenty years of observing the career trajectories of thousands of professionals—from Fortune 500 CEOs to millennials just starting out. During a few long flights to Asia and Europe, I finally wrote up an article for FastCompany. com called "Career Rocket Fuel" that was later posted on LinkedIn, SlideShare, and Twitter. To my shock, it garnered over 50,000 views.

So, after twenty years, it finally dawned on me that there is a deep and growing hunger for practical modern advice on how to think about careers. Our colleges, graduate schools, and companies may teach the world's greatest technical and business skills. But talented, smart people everywhere are still confused and frustrated because they don't know how to put all the advice, insights, and best practices together into a cohesive career plan. This doesn't surprise me at all. The world of jobs and careers is almost unrecognizable compared to just a decade ago. Many of the job-search techniques and career strategies that worked in previous generations simply don't work today. There are some great long-term principles that still hold true, but people in today's career marketplace face some unique challenges.

The Long View is broken into three main sections. Part One introduces you to the right career mindset, framework, and tools. Here you learn about the critical importance of "fuel" in the context of your career. You'll learn ways to think about your long-term career horizon, how to invest your time, how to expand your personal network, and a framework to use when facing tough career decisions. The tools you read about in this book are ones that I've developed as I've charted my own course. They are exercises that I still do regularly and refer to often. I have shared them with friends and colleagues and their enthusiasm has encouraged me to refine and develop them in the hopes that they will be of value to you.

Part Two gives you practical advice and examples throughout the three main stages of a career. Here we will learn about the experiences of individuals at different career stages and in different industries—some success stories and some cautionary tales. Along the way, you will hear dozens of stories from interesting people like twenty-eight-year-old Mohammed Ashour, the star McGill University MBA student who is betting the first stage of his career on a start-up that breeds insects for food, Rachel S. Moore, who went from a teenage ballerina to one of the leading CEOs in the world of art and music, and Tim Penner, the former president of P&G Canada, who found a new passion for nonprofit work after the age of fifty-five.

Part Three puts it in all in the context of real life, including topics like balancing your career strategy with parenthood, international relocation, and dealing with career setbacks. Careers aren't always convenient, or perfectly timed. How do you cope with the inevitable messiness that life will throw at you?

The Long View lands on the ultimate question: Are careers about success or happiness? To me, it's not just about finding work you love, but building a life that you love as well. Happiness at work and job satisfaction are terms that have been thrown around for decades. And today, top authors like Tom Rath, Dan Pink, and Adam Grant bring us consistent evidence that happiness at work translates to increased productivity, health, and a host of other benefits. Most career books focus on just one aspect: the job. But the reality many of us know today includes a blurred line between our lives at work and our lives at home.

We need a work philosophy that encompasses all the parts of our lives, and one that can give us guidance on how to be ambitious and seek success without sacrificing other things we value deeply—family, friends, health, and purpose. This book is about building a long-term plan, because we all know that the things that brought us happiness in our twenties and thirties will change and evolve as we continue our professional trajectories. We need a set of tools that will change and grow with us, which take into account how big life moments can alter your perspective and change your goals.

My sincere hope is that *The Long View* will in some way spur you to the strongest, highest, longest, and happiest career possible. I have had the pleasure and privilege of working with some of the top companies in the world—including IBM, American Express, Procter & Gamble,

IKEA, Nestle, Unilever, Facebook, Google, Yahoo!, BlackRock Financial Group, and Coca-Cola. As a CEO, I have hired, fired, and counseled thousands of employees on their careers over the past three decades. In researching for this book, I have met some of the world's most accomplished entrepreneurs, academics, artists, athletes, and community volunteers. *The Long View* is intended to spark the kind of conversations that aren't happening often enough in schools and companies today.

In *The Long View*, I will offer the advice that I would take myself if I were starting out today. It's the advice I give to emerging leaders as they approach their primes. It's the advice I am taking right now as I contemplate the next phase of my own career. And it is the advice I offer my two Millennial-aged daughters as they embark on the long, scary, and exhilarating career journey ahead.

1

PRINCIPLES
AND TOOLS

CHAPTER 1

Executive Summary:
The Long View Career Method

The Problem

In the course of over thirty-five years in global business, I have seen tens of thousands of career trajectories, from CEOs of Fortune 500 companies, to mid-level professionals entering their primes, to twenty-two year olds just starting out.

Here is what I've found: most people have the wrong approach to careers. The majority across all age groups think of their work life as a job, not a career. Too much focus is placed on the immediate next step, not the pathway. Most treat a career like a sprint, when, in fact, it is a forty-five-plus-year marathon. They are more focused on getting promoted on Tuesday than on having great choices when it really matters—when they are in their forties and fifties. Many are deeply worried about their careers, and are seeking advice, but finding few answers. The notion of a career is changing fast, and it is hard to rely on what has worked in the past. As a result, too many people hop around aimlessly, or get stuck in unrewarding work, seemingly unable to break out of a rut. They need a plan. You need a plan.

Five Things You Need to Know to Build a Career Plan

1. Careers last a surprisingly long time, and embrace three distinctly different stages. Careers last much longer than people think—forty-five years or more—and are likely to get even longer in the future. For most people, there are more years of career *after* the age of forty than before. Careers consist of three major stages, each lasting about fifteen years. The three stages are highly interconnected, and what you do in one stage creates opportunities and consequences in later stages. You will learn more about the career stages in chapter 2.

Stage One is the time to start strong. Your career efforts must be focused on discovery and equipping yourself for the long journey ahead. Your learning curve is more important than your job title. Create the foundation for your career and establish good early habits. In chapter 8, we dive deeper into Stage One and learn hands-on lessons on how to get in the game and get off to a powerful start.

Stage Two is the time to reach high. The prime objective for this stage is to find your sweet spot—the intersection of what you're good at, what you love to do, and what the world appreciates. It is the time to differentiate yourself from the pack, to stand out, and to become eligible for career pathways that will be most rewarding to you. Focus on your strengths and largely ignore your weaknesses. For more tactics and stories on Stage Two, see chapter 9.

Stage Three is devoted to achieving lasting impact and finding a sustainable new career pathway that will likely need to last well into your sixties or even seventies. You have three critical jobs in Stage Three: pass the torch to the next generation, stay relevant, and ignite a new career flame for yourself.

2. "Fuel" is important—it matters what you build on. In order to propel yourself through the long journey, you will need abundant supplies of career fuel. This fuel comes in three main forms: transportable skills, meaningful experiences, and enduring relationships. Without this fuel, you risk becoming fragile and vulnerable as the global workplace continues to shift in unpredictable ways. Fuel is critical throughout your career. In Stage One you need to accumulate it, in Stage Two you need to take advantage of it, and in Stage Three you need to refresh and preserve it. Learn more about the various forms of fuel in chapter 3.

3. Careers are built through the skillful investment of time. It takes patience and persistence to build sustainable fuel levels. Becoming a highly employable expert or "master" is not just the result of innate talent, but of the application of thousands of hours of learning, experience, and practice. How you invest your time in work and in life has a profound impact on your success and happiness.

4. Careers do not progress in linear or predictable ways. You must remain in constant discovery and learning mode. Career opportunities will evolve, and your own life goals will change. When you are confronted with new pathways and opportunities, remain calm and think strategically. Be prepared to embrace the inevitable changes and adjust your career strategy accordingly. Successful careers are a combination of diligent planning and good luck. The diligent planning is essential, because it makes you eligible for the luck.

5. A career is so much more than a job: it's a big part of life. That is why you need a career-planning framework that doesn't just compare jobs, but takes a holistic approach to how your career fits in with your broader life ambitions—parenthood, global travel, your future, and ultimately your happiness. You owe yourself a career strategy and a plan. And there is no question about who needs to take accountability for that plan. There are over seven billion people on the planet, and only one of them will be with you throughout your entire career. It's you.

Five Things You Need to Do to Bring Your Career Plan to Life

You cannot wish your way to career happiness. You need to do some homework.

1. Do the Career Math exercise to get into the right long-term frame of mind. See chapter 4 (page 51) for the simple but provocative questions that will help you appreciate the big picture for long-range career planning.

2. Complete a Career Inventory to take stock of your most relevant skills, experiences and relationships. As part of the inventory, assess what career stage you are at, and map out your career ecosystem—the connections, communities, colleagues and champions who are critical to your career success. Establish your career goals and conduct an annual progress report based on four golden questions—in the next year, what are you looking for most: Learning, Impact, Fun, or Rewards? See chapter 5 (page 56).

3. Take the 100-Hour Test and complete a Personal Time Portfolio to see how you are investing your time. Are you devoting enough time to the things that make you most successful and happy? See chapter 6 (page 73).

4. Use the Career Path Navigator when you are trying to set a new career pathway or decide between several options. See chapter 7 (page 83).

5. Future-proof your career by periodically challenging yourself with the five scary long-term questions explored in the final chapter (page 218).

- How can I avoid being replaced by a machine?
- Where and how will I find work?
- How will I spend my time in the future?
- Will I outlive my money?
- How will work make me happy?

Visit **thelongviewcareer.com** to find downloadable and printable copies of all of these exercises, along with helpful extra content and resources.

The Result

If you embrace these five principles and complete the five exercises, you will be far better equipped than the vast majority of people in the workplace. The act of planning puts you more in control of your destiny. It means less worry and more action. You will build a more robust foundation for the future. You will give yourself your best shot at happiness in your career and your life.

CHAPTER 2

The Three Big Career Stages

There are three big stages of a career, each lasting about fifteen years, and each with its own dominant strategy.

- Stage One—Start strong by taking on fuel
- Stage Two—Reach high by focusing on your strengths and passions
- Stage Three—Go far by staying fresh and then passing the torch

In many ways, building a career is like building a brand. You need a great product, built on quality ingredients. It needs to stand for something. It needs to be nurtured and refreshed to evolve over time. And just as the discipline of brand building is changing these days, so is career building. It is more interactive and participatory than ever before. You need to design for robustness and agility. In a world that is more and more transparent, you cannot hide bad ingredients or bad construction.

Stage One: Start Strong by Taking on Fuel

The whole purpose of the first fifteen years of your career is to lay the foundation for the next two stages. Stage One is not just about being patient; it is about taking action that will pay dividends down the road. This is the time to get into the game. It is the time to discover what you are good at and what you love to do. It is the time to establish good early work habits. Most importantly, it is the time to build your fuel supply. Too many people do not spend enough time building their skills, experiences, and relationships early on. As a result, they run out of momentum midway through their careers, just when it should be getting the most interesting and rewarding.

Stage One is the time to explore and heal your weaknesses. If you are terrible at public speaking, take improv classes. If you are too tough or too weak with team members, get personal leadership coaching. Learning is more important than unadulterated success. It is okay to fail sometimes, as long as you learn and apply those lessons to future victories.

Stage Two: Reach High by Focusing on Your Strengths

Stage Two is the time to find the intersection zone between what you are good at, what you love to do, and what the world appreciates. Stage Two (perhaps fifteen years into your career) is the time to define your sweet spot, set a high ambition, pour fuel onto your strengths, and differentiate yourself from the pack.

Build on your core strengths and push yourself to make them great. By the time you are into Stage Two, it is very hard to fix weaknesses. It is often much better to stay focused on your strengths and surround yourself with people who complement you and compensate for the things you do not do as well. No top leader does it all. If you are good at strategy and vision, you may need an operations wizard by your side. If you are great at execution, you may need someone who is more creative and visionary on your team. Own up to your shortcomings, cast around them, and spend most of your time on your core strengths.

If you are a good communicator, work to become the best public speaker in your company. If you are a talented connector, take on tough team challenges that show your special abilities to integrate where others have failed. If you are a highly effective doer, then celebrate it. Stand for something that others value. Fly your flag. You are a career brand. You are on the shelf with other competent and well-intentioned brands. Some boss with a job opening or promotion is shopping for a solution to their problem and you need to get them to pick you.

Stage Three: Go Far by Passing the Torch and Reigniting the Flame

Traditionally, the last years of a career were marked by a distinct fall-off (retirement day) or a sad drift. In my view, the third stage of a career can be exceptionally fulfilling and enduring. But it takes the right mindset and expectations and preparation. The primary purpose of Stage Three is to pass the torch: closing the loop on succession planning and evolving from a doing/leading role to an advisory/contributory role. This is where the student becomes the teacher, the mentee becomes the mentor, and the leader becomes the valued contributor.

Succession: How do I equip the next generation in my company to succeed? This can range from a simple, thoughtful hand-off of duties and lessons learned to a much more formal hand-over of leadership or ownership.

Consultancy and paid advisory boards: Consulting jobs and board appointments can be great Stage Three gigs if you can get them. But you need to have laid the tracks in Stage Two to get asked. These roles are in hot demand now as Boomers age out of the traditional workforce in record numbers. The tight competition means that nobody owes you a paid consultancy or board position. You need to earn it.

Entrepreneurship: Starting up your own small venture is not only for the young. For many people in the latter stages of their careers, entrepreneurship is becoming a viable and exciting option. With e-commerce, the barriers to getting started are lower than ever.

Teaching: To me, teaching is a critical part of a rewarding Stage Three experience. Think broadly about what you know and who you could teach. You can aim as loftily as a college professorship or as down-to-earth as tutoring local kids to read. Adult schools offer hundreds of courses in business, the arts, languages, life skills, hobbies, and crafts. What tribal wisdom do you have to pass along?

Community: Recent retirees often talk about their hopes of "sitting on a few community boards," but they are startled to find how competitive and demanding these roles can be. Frankly, I wouldn't want someone on my board who wants to sit around and preside. But I would absolutely welcome a volunteer who says they want to "contribute to this exciting mission." You need to be productive. Do things. Contribute, or you won't be asked back.

To be effective in Stage Three you must stay fresh and relevant. People value history, but only to the extent that it informs present-day conditions and challenges. If you don't stay at least broadly informed and relevant, don't expect people to listen to you. And certainly not to hire you. Staying relevant is part of your job in Stage Three.

CHAPTER 3

Fuel

"Your vehicle of leadership is fueled by your
willingness to learn." —Israelmore Ayivor

As a CEO and career advisor, I see it constantly; people underestimate the length of the journey and run out of fuel. Many people focus on the trappings of careers: titles, promotions, office space, salaries, and awards. These can be important milestones, but they are not the end game. If there is one thing you remember from reading this book, it should be that truly successful long-term careers are propelled by fuel. The smart strategy is to accumulate fuel throughout your career, to constantly refresh it, and to expend it wisely.

There are three essential forms of fuel in a career, and each one is important to long-term success.

- Transportable skills
- Meaningful experiences
- Enduring relationships

Fuel #1: Transportable Skills

Transportable skills are fundamental abilities that you will acquire and carry with you throughout your career. They are not just technical knowledge and jargon that help you to do your current job. They are capabilities and building blocks that you will carry with you from job to job, company to company, and even industry to industry. Here are some examples of transportable skills that I have found really make a difference:

Problem-solving: At some level, every single job in the world exists to solve a problem. Can you assess a problem and create a plan? When you are given a challenge and a blank piece of paper, do you have a solid method or two that you can rely on to help solve the problem? I had the good fortune to work at Procter & Gamble early in my career. They gave me a solid grounding in methods and principles that have served me well throughout my work life. From my Ogilvy & Mather training and client experience, I have learned others.

One of the approaches I use in business—whether I am talking to a CEO or a new employee—is to start with "how do customers shop for this product or service?" I have heard other people ask "how would Google or Apple tackle this problem?" Trained scientists or accountants might also have their own preferred method. In interview situations, I always throw candidates at least one open-ended question that is almost impossible to answer. I am not so interested in whether they get the question correct. I am always interested in how they attack the problem. The good news is that there are many frameworks and strategies to help you improve your problem-solving abilities. Be intentional in adding several different approaches to your repertoire, and don't be afraid to combine a few different methods to create something unique that works for you. What is *your* method? Where are you learning to be a better and more robust problem solver?

Persuasive communication: The ability to persuade is a critical lifelong skill, regardless of what industry you end up in. Inventors and creative people need to sell their ideas. Doctors need to convince others of their diagnoses. Businesspeople need to sell their products and services. Community volunteers and activists need to win supporters for their missions. Musicians and artists need to win jobs and recruit fans. Whether you're speaking to a client, a colleague, a friend, or a stranger—being able to present your point of view in a clear and concise manner is an essential skill. Some people find persuasion shallow or distasteful. Get over it. There are so many different styles—from the strong and flashy closer to the quiet credible adviser. Susan Cain, in her outstanding book *Quiet*, illuminates the hidden power of the introvert. Whether you are a natural extrovert or an introvert, find your own style, but *do* learn how to persuade. In my experience, the people who cannot convince others of their ideas become frustrated and undervalued in their careers.

In today's work environment, persuasive communication needs to be expressed through many different channels. How good are you at expressing yourself in writing? Can you articulate a crisp written point of view, supported by a few good reasons to believe you? When you try to convince someone in an e-mail, how often does it come back with the reply "Got it, thanks"? Or do your e-mails tend to ignite an e-mail war? Can you persuade in person, one-on-one? Can you speak in front of a group and move them to action? Today, one of the world's greatest persuasion channels is the online video. Could you do a two-minute video on a topic you are passionate about and attract more than a thousand views (without taking your clothes off)? You should actually try it in the next six months. Pick a topic, shoot a low-cost video, post it, and see what happens. Try some variations. Nothing will hone your storytelling faster than getting views, likes, and shares from a real audience.

One of the things you'll learn by testing your storytelling skills is that simplicity wins. So many people, especially early in their careers, believe that jargon, complex language, and acronyms make them sound smarter. In fact, it has the opposite effect. Jargon and complex words don't win an audience; they lose it. Use words and images that people understand and can get excited about. Sometimes, when I have a complex problem to solve, I do an exercise I call "write a letter to Mom." I literally draft out a letter to my mother explaining the issues and what I am thinking of doing. Since my mother has never worked in my industry, the exercise forces me to keep the language extremely simple and the key points exceptionally clear. Try writing a "letter to Mom" next time you are facing a tough challenge.

Persuasion is not just opinions expressed loudly. That might work once, but it doesn't work over the long haul. Part of being persuasive is bringing forward compelling facts that truly give people permission to believe you. I worry that in the world of ubiquitous information, there are too many opinions and half-truths available, but too few authoritative sources. When I work with young professionals at my company I always encourage them to back up every key point with a footnote and a source. It is an old-school method that still works incredibly well today. When you go to the effort of finding authoritative sources and documenting them, it signals to your audience that you've done your homework and have conviction behind your point of view.

A few years ago, I did a research paper called "The Future of Selling." We found that while a few lucky people are gifted "natural salespeople," for most of us this skill must be developed. When I left Procter & Gamble, I was really good at expressing my point of view in a tight two-page written recommendation, because that was P&G's preferred method of communication. But when I moved on from P&G, I found I was utterly hopeless at public speaking. Any time I tried to address more than about four people, I was paralyzed from the top of my head to the base of my spine. If I didn't fix it, I'd be pretty useless in my job. I took some company training and put in my practice hours. I tried to do at least one public speaking event every week—even if it was announcing someone's birthday in front of a small crowd at work. Eventually, I became comfortable in larger crowds and in different forums. Today, you can barely shut me up. I still practice and still rehearse and still get nervous before every presentation. For formal speeches, I put in at least five hours of preparation time for every twenty minutes of stage time. If you are not sure that you can communicate persuasively in person, in writing, on stage and on camera—take it on as a fundamental career challenge, and start putting in the time now.

• • •

The last thing that is often overlooked in communication has nothing to do with the person speaking at all. One of the best skills to learn is the ability to spot communication breakdowns and adjust your approach accordingly. There are a few different things that can go wrong during a conversation:

- Correspondence is when two people use different words to say the same thing. Have you ever been having a conversation and right after you finish speaking, someone makes the same point you just made but with different words? That's correspondence.
- Conflict can arise when two people use the same word but mean different things. This comes up a lot when talking about abstract concepts like "efficiency" or "quality." Even "punctual" can mean different things depending on the cultural context. Being on time for a meeting in the Middle East versus Germany can be wildly different.
- Contrast happens where there is no overlap at all. This is when two colleagues cannot seem to see eye to eye.

You can be a wonderfully persuasive and comfortable public speaker, but if you can't analyze the situation and quickly adjust your strategy, you might run into some difficulties.

Getting things done: The ability to execute and get things done is so basic, but of immense value in the context of your long career. Everybody can execute to some extent, but it's the ones who consistently deliver—through thick and thin—who really stand out. Can you not only start but also finish projects—consistently? Have you learned how to power through to achieve the end goal, regardless of the barriers and obstacles thrown at you? Are people at work trusting you with more and more high-profile projects, or are those being assigned to others? If you can deliver once, it's a heroic act. If you can deliver consistently, it is a powerful lifelong career skill. Hunt down the people in your organization who own the best reputations for getting stuff done, and learn from the best. Do, learn, repeat.

Becoming a talent magnet: They say that the companies with the best people always win. I agree. And it is also true that the individual leaders who have the ability to attract and mobilize top talent win. Having great talent around you enables you in your job, and amplifies your impact. It is one of the factors that separate the good from the great. "Talent magnets" don't just perform at a higher level as individuals— they nurture and develop the next generation of stars, and attract fresh talent into the organization.

Being a talent magnet starts with having the right mind-set: ultimately, no one needs to work for you, they must *want* to work for you. I call it the "eBay factor"—if you were put up on eBay and employees needed to bid for the pleasure of working for you, who would bid? Would it be the mediocre approval-seekers, or the rising stars? Maybe no one would bid. Do you make work more challenging and fun? Do you teach your staff valuable skills that will propel them forward? Do you treat people fairly and transparently?

Most of us don't start our careers with a lot of direct reports. Some career paths—like doctor or sole proprietor—may never have too many employees. But each of us can use the talent "moments of truth" to create a transportable skill. A moment of truth arises every time you are faced with an opportunity to hire, fire, promote, transfer, or give a raise to someone. How you perform in these moments defines your skill as a talent magnet. If you're at a junior level, you can still use the experiences you have with your bosses to identify the things that made you feel valued and the things you want to avoid when you're further along. There are lessons everywhere.

I encourage young leaders to evaluate their "talent ledger" after they have been in the workforce for a few years. Take a look at each of their moments of truth and try to assess whether their action resulted in a plus or a minus in their talent ledger. For example, when they hired their first assistant, was that a good talent decision or a poor one? Did that individual perform well and progress within the firm, or flame out? When faced with a tough decision on who to give a scarce promotion or salary increase to, did the leader back the right pony? Did they lean forward on the capable, high-potential candidate, or cave in to the squeaky wheel?

A leader's talent ledger emerges over time with lots of pluses and minuses along the way, but I find it is a powerful predictor of career success. I include a talent ledger conversation every time I evaluate one of our senior leaders. I ask candidates for senior roles to tell me about the people who worked for them at various companies in the past. Where did you find the people—did you inherit them or recruit them? Most importantly, where are they now? Did they thrive within that firm or the industry? Did the best ones follow you to your next company? The worst answer someone can give me is, "Good question. I don't know where they are now." This signals to me that the person is someone who doesn't deeply value talent, and is likely deficient in the critical "talent magnet" skill. What does *your* talent ledger look like? How will you take advantage of the next precious talent moments of truth to make your ledger even stronger?

Giving and asking for help: In his best-selling book *Give and Take*, Adam Grant presents compelling evidence that becoming a successful "Giver" can make you much more effective in business and life. Many people find it counterintuitive, but Grant has the research and the examples to back it up. Grant looked at three relationship styles and correlated them to work performance and happiness measures. "Taking" is a pattern of asking without giving back, "matching" is giving, but with the expectation of getting something in return, and "giving" is unconditional giving with no major expectation of receiving something back. Givers are net exporters of help and are high in the attributes of helpfulness, responsibility, social justice, and compassion. According to Grant, successful Givers—those who give more than they take—are much more likely to be among the highest performing and most satisfied people.

I have also seen what Grant sees—highly effective executives who have the ability to give in a way that amplifies their impact and brings out the best in others. The more selfish "taking" style is tempting—and can often work for a period of time. But as Grant observes—and I see it, too—as the world becomes more transparent and careers become longer, more and more Takers will be exposed. And the Givers will ascend. In my experience, people gravitate toward leaders they can trust. And "giving" behavior is a powerful way to build that trust. Learning how to ask for help and, most importantly, how to give it will become a great transportable career skill for the long haul.

Emotional intelligence (aka EQ): In my business, I always look for evidence of emotional intelligence—something that suggests a high emotional quotient (aka EQ). It's your ability to understand and connect to people's emotional states—for example, reading the body language of someone who is uncomfortable or angry, or knowing how to interpret social cues, moods, and nonverbal signals from those around you. Daniel Goleman is a pioneer in the field of emotional intelligence. In his book *Working with Emotional Intelligence*, Goleman argues that the single most important factor in job performance and advancement is emotional intelligence. Through his access to business leaders around the world and studies in more than five hundred organizations, Goleman documents an astonishing fact: in determining star performance in every field, emotional intelligence matters twice as much as IQ or technical expertise. For leaders, emotional intelligence is almost 90 percent of what sets stars apart from the mediocre.

Building EQ is a real issue and also a real opportunity for career-minded people. I received a request from a young man named Raymond who had just started his career as business analyst with a leading global consulting company.

He had recently graduated as a top student in the field of nanoscience and had done a couple of science and analytics-oriented internships. He asked me a really good question. Given his scientific background and analytical bent, did I think it was worthwhile for him to actively develop his "EQ." Is building EQ worth it? And if so, how should he go about it? I think Raymond is being really really smart. Adding EQ to his strong cognitive skills will give him a big leg up as he rises up through world of consulting, science, or whatever he pursues.

I don't have all the answers, but here's the practical advice I offered to Raymond: I encouraged him take on building his EQ as a two-year assignment for personal development. I absolutely believe that it will help distinguish him from other book-smart people in his field and increase his chance of long-term success. I recommended a couple of top books to read on the subject including Dan Goleman's *Working With Emotional Intelligence*, and *Emotional Intelligence 2.0* by Bradberry and Greaves. But for Raymond, the book learning will be the easy part. He must create hands-on experiences that help him identify and hone his EQ skills. He should sign up for team leadership experiences in his company and his industry. He needs to explicitly ask for feedback from colleagues on his emotional leadership, and learn that it is not just the emotional signals he intends to send that matter, but what signals are actually received by his audience. He should become a keen observer of people around him who are good (or bad) at managing the emotional side of business. I encouraged Raymond to take notes on what leaders in his company did and said in interpersonal situations and identify what's working and what's not. I told him to do as much public speaking as possible; seeing how a live audience responds is a rich learning experience. He should continue to travel outside his home city, and outside his comfort zone. And if he really wants to make progress, Raymond should sign up for improvisation or theater classes. Even if he finds it awkward, nothing will push him faster to understand the emotional landscape, how to react to it, and how to navigate through it. Building EQ may take several years of hard work, but it's totally worth it.

Here are three more of my favorite "transportable skills" that are dead simple, but will last a lifetime.

1. How to look people in the eye and shake their hand. A friend of mine who now runs a real estate development company recounts one of the lifelong skills he picked up at college. "In my final year playing basketball at college, our coach gave us the greatest lesson ever. He said we would meet a lot of important people in our senior years as athletes, and throughout our lives. So instead of practicing layup shots or dribbling, we spent the entire practice saying hello, looking people in the eye, and shaking their hands. Absolutely priceless." I find it shocking when I interview people and they struggle to look me squarely in the eye, or worse, fidget with their phones.

2. How to search. Everybody uses search engines to find answers. Most are lousy at it. They don't know how to corroborate their findings. They don't know how to discriminate between the authoritative sources and the bozo ones. They do not know how to express data in a clear and persuasive manner. I give people small tasks all the time to go find a specific fact or source. I am amazed at how differently people perform the tasks. The ones who are highly effective searchers will have an advantage for their whole careers.

3. How to breathe. Work requires us to be focused and relaxed. I took a few courses way back at the beginning of my career that taught the basics of breathing and relaxation. I still use some of the techniques today before big speeches and meetings. These simple lessons were incredibly useful, and I wish I had done more.

Transportable skills form the foundation of your career skill set. They are transportable because you can carry them with you from job to job and company to company. It is essential that some of the skills you acquire are transportable because, on average, a person will work in over twelve to fifteen different jobs during their careers (Department of Labor/Forbes/Forrester Research), and 80 percent of students entering high school will end up in jobs that do not exist today.

Fuel #2: Meaningful Experiences

Meaningful experiences combine to enable you to be versatile and robust in your career. New experiences take you outside your comfort zone and build new career muscles. I tend to avoid candidates who may only thrive only in one kind of controlled environment, like a hothouse flower. Instead, I look for diverse experiences in a candidate's background to make sure that they are adaptable and agile.

A colleague of mine, Rory Sutherland, is a noted speaker and thought leader on the subject of behavioral change. Rory notes that "variance"—i.e. trying things in different environments and experimenting with different ways of doing things—creates more robust decision-making skills. If we always do things the same way, we become very efficient, but fragile. In genetics, we know that embracing some level of genetic diversity and mutation creates a more vigorous species. Maybe it is better to become a "career mutt" with plenty of diverse experiences, than a "career thoroughbred" who can only do one thing.

Do not let your career become fragile. As your career develops, look for opportunities to work in a corporate environment and an entrepreneurial one, work in a foreign country (or at least a few different cities), launch something new, manage through a crisis, and put on a major event or show where there is visible risk of personal failure.

In my business, many careers have been built in the crucible of big product launches and new business pitches. These assignments are intense and deadline-driven. They force people out of their comfort zones and get them to feel the flop-sweat of possible failure. Find assignments where there is skin in the game. Put your hand up and break new ground.

Mark Linaugh is the head of talent at the world's largest communications company, WPP, responsible for nearly

200,000 staff. When he is looking to hire or promote a new leader, he wants to see evidence of leadership versatility.

- Have they started up something?
- Have they rapidly expanded a business?
- Have they turned around a struggling business and made it healthy?

As we'll discuss later on, this doesn't necessarily mean you need to jump around from company to company looking to acquire new experiences. If you express your openness and are a bit patient, you can often find tremendous diversity of experience within the same firm. Early on in my career, I was offered the chance to lead a small entrepreneurial division of Ogilvy & Mather in Canada. On the surface, it was not at all a sexy assignment, and several others had turned it down. After several sleepless nights, I decided to accept the job, and it was one of the best decisions of my career. At first, people wondered what I had done wrong to be relegated to this unglamorous job, but over time it gave me incredible early exposure to all kinds of business situations and problems. Four years later, when there was an opening for the top job in Canada, I was appointed specifically because I had gone though the trials and tribulations of that unsexy sidestep. The lessons I learned in that seemingly unappetizing job are still paying dividends more than twenty years later.

Many people ask me about career pathways that have a great future. There are hundreds of viable options, but I confess that I have a favorite. I think that everybody in business these days should spend at least one chapter of their career working in e-commerce—even if it's just for a couple of years. Here's why: e-commerce is a huge industry with great long-term prospects. It is already worth hundreds of billions of dollars and is projected to grow over 15 percent per year over the next decade. Because e-commerce involves the whole selling process, it teaches you to think like a general manager—from product development to how the supply chain works to merchandising, customer service, and more. It gives you exposure to the "soft skills" of business like branding and customer experience as well as the "hard skills" of profit management, data, and analytics. Best of all, a job in e-commerce means that you get a report card every day in the form of immediate sales. E-commerce can act like a microcosm of all business in a single job assignment. What a fantastic way to accelerate your learning and development. If I were starting my career over today, I would spend at least one chapter doing e-commerce.

So, whether it is entrepreneurial experience, a second language, an international assignment, a volunteer project, or a chapter of e-commerce, a steady diet of meaningful experiences builds a stronger career. Be open to them. Volunteer for them. Embrace them as part of your long journey.

Fuel #3: Enduring Relationships

Enduring relationships are perhaps the most potent and long-lasting form of fuel. They include both the brands you associate with and the people you connect with throughout the journey. Collectively, they form your career ecosystem, which you will learn more about in chapter 5.

The employers you work for have always mattered,

and they matter more now than ever before. Whether you work for a conventional Fortune 500 company, a start-up, or a foreign-owned firm, search engines like Google and social platforms like LinkedIn now make your employment brands visible to the world. Are you proud of the companies you have worked for? What do they say about you? What reputation do you carry forward (positive or negative) because you worked at company X and company Y? If you want to see what employer brands carry the best reputations, consult sources like the WPP Brandz list of the World's Most Valuable Brands or Fortune's Most Admired Companies. Every company you work for may not be famous, but make sure that they are respected.

Personal relationships are every bit as important. All kinds of them. They include:

> **Your bosses.** This is the number one relationship you will experience. No one has more impact (for better or for worse) than your immediate boss. Are you learning best practices and good habits? Are you working for a respected career professional who is going places? Have you learned from an entrepreneur who will teach you about risk-taking and other transportable skills?

> **Clients/customer relationships.** These personal connections can be crucial in any career—but especially for those in marketing, sales, or professional services. It sends a powerful message when your clients and customers value you so much they follow you around as you move into different roles, firms, or even industries. The "eBay factor"

I mentioned in the section on talent magnetism can also be applied to client relationships. I often ask my Ogilvy leaders: "If you were put up on eBay, what clients would "bid" for you and ask for you by name?"

Business partners. Are you working with excellent business partners such as consultants, agency partners, technology vendors, or talent recruiters who can support and propel your career down the road? Jobs later in your career can be scary and lonely. As a senior person, you often feel like you need to know all the answers, and your peers can sometimes be your competitors. It is great to have a roster of talented and supportive partners on your side.

Talent around you. Are you meeting top-rate leaders and subject-matter experts early in your career? Here's a good question to ask yourself: "If I started my own company, who from around here would I want to bring with me (and would they come if I asked them)?"

Find your tribe. In the past, many professional networks were built around clubs. Increasingly, they are built around communities. Check out professional networks at work and explore digital communities like Summit and Ten Thousand Coffees. You may find them very rich in opportunities to build your skills and relationships.

Fuel—Summary

There are several reasons why we need these three fuels in such abundant supply. First of all, they give us choices— what the behavioral economists call "optionality." You do not want to build yourself a skill set that can only work in one firm, or one industry, or one city. Having deep foundational skills makes us eligible for different and bigger roles. Whether we choose to pursue them or not is a different matter, but having this fuel on board puts us in the game. Second, these kinds of fuel build our self-reliance. Industries and companies are forming and breaking up every day. None of us can predict exactly what the job market will look like in five years, let alone in a decade or four decades. We need to be nimble. Here is a great theoretical exercise suggested by social scientist Charles Handy: Imagine if at the age of forty you had to quit your job forever and start a company with just you. What would you do? That is a great test of self-reliance.

Finally, these grades of fuel give us longevity. A person starting out today needs enough juice to remain relevant and employable for an average of at *least* forty years. And as we'll learn later in chapter 14, this horizon could stretch much further out. Load up.

CHAPTER 4

The Career Math Exercise

"I've learned that finishing a marathon isn't just an athletic achievement. It's a state of mind; a state of mind that says anything is possible." —John Hanc, marathon runner and writer

Start With Career Math

To start building a career plan, you need to be in the right mind-set. To get into that mind-set, you need to start with a bit of math.

1. Take the number sixty-two and deduct your current age. This is the number of years you have left until *early* retirement. The median age of retirement in the US is sixty-two and it is similar or a bit older in most Western markets.[3] For the

---

3   See Gallup research 2014 and 2015 for retirement trends. For most recent data and long-term trends, see Gallup.com.

past twenty years, the retirement age has been rising, and the trend is likely to continue. For many people, the chief reason is that social security and pension benefits are being systematically reduced or deferred. Others are putting off retirement by choice because they are enjoying good health and interesting work later into their sixties and seventies. Whatever the reason, for most of us retirement will come at age sixty-two or later, and we need to come to grips with that. If today you are in your late twenties, you have almost thirty-five years of your career left. Many people think that careers are pretty much over at forty. Even if you are forty, you are not even at the halfway point. Most people vastly underestimate the length of a career.

2. How many hours does it take to become truly "excellent" at something? In his book *Outliers*, Malcolm Gladwell studied super-performers in various fields such as sports, music, art, and business. He estimated that it takes about 10,000 hours of intense practice and rehearsal to become excellent at something. As Gladwell observes:

"Once a musician has enough ability to get into a top music school, the thing that distinguishes one performer from another is how hard he or she works. That's it. And what's more, the people at the very top don't just work harder or even much harder than everyone else. They work much, much harder.... Achievement is talent plus preparation. Practice isn't the thing you do once you're good. It's the thing you do that makes you good."

The key point is that innate talent is not enough. No matter how many IQ points or natural gifts you have, being successful takes intense hard work and many more hours than you think. Take a look at the industry that you're interested in. Research other people's trajectories and you'll start to find that there is a certain amount of time you have to spent acquiring key skills and experience. This can vary from industry to industry and from person to person—the idea is to understand the investment you'll need to make in order to move forward. Consider that Jiro Ono, considered to be one of the world's top sushi chefs won't let his apprentices cook anything until they've spent ten years mastering their knives. The more you know about the skills you need to acquire the better prepared you'll be to make the best decisions in your career that will maximize your long-term success.

3. What percentage of your personal wealth do you accumulate after your fortieth birthday? Most people guess about 60 percent. Young people tend to guess smaller percentages like 40 percent. The real answer is actually 85-90 percent. An individual's personal wealth tends to peak at about age sixty-five, and their personal wealth at age forty is only about 10-15 percent of that amount.[4] The *vast* majority of personal wealth accumulation occurs after the age of forty. The reasons are pretty simple. First, as we learned earlier, you have more years of career earnings after age forty than before, and they tend to be the higher-paying ones. Second, you enjoy the effects of compound interest. And third, many expenses tend to taper off once mortgages and child-related expenses are covered. It is true that personal wealth can decline later in life (especially after eighty due to health-care

---

4   The latest Survey of Consumer Finances (based on 2013 census) gives median net worth at age forty as $38,500. Median net worth at the peak (age sixty-five) is $309,000.

expenses), but the big point is that the wealth accumulation game for most people is heavily back-end loaded into the forties, fifties and even sixties. Most people totally miss this.

4. How many Facebook friends and LinkedIn contacts do you have? The purpose of this question is to understand how much "social currency" people think they have based on the number of social and business relationships they have acquired. The answers I get to question number four are always in the hundreds, and often in the thousands, especially among young people. The median number of Facebook friends per active adult user is about two hundred, and among eighteen to twenty-five year olds it is three hundred. The average number of LinkedIn contacts is 339. Many people think that the key to a successful career is to have the *most* social contacts. But as we'll see below and in the chapter on career ecosystems, that is not the whole story.

5. How many people do you think you will meet in "career heaven"—those people who will really make a difference to your career and life? Of course, there is no one correct answer to this question, but I use it to compare and contrast with question number four. In my experience, when people reflect on their long careers at awards dinners and retirement parties, they often focus on a few individuals who made a major mark on their careers. They don't say, "I'd like to thank my 1,632 LinkedIn connections." They say, "There are three (or four or five) special people who made it all possible."

We all discover people in the course of our careers who become our mentors, teachers, and advocates. They are the people who champion us and say nice things about us behind our backs. They nominate us for jobs and awards.

Even people in their early twenties probably already have at least one mentor in their lives. Who was the person who recommended you for college? Or that person who proposed you for your first job or promotion? Over time, additional mentors will emerge and, occasionally, some will fade. But always remember there is someone out there who is in your corner.

What Does This Career Math Mean?

The big and stunningly obvious conclusion is that a career is a long journey, often lasting more than forty-five years. Most people vastly underestimate how long a career is and miss opportunities as a result. Like a marathon runner, you need ambition, a plan, some preparation, and a smart sense of pacing. You need nourishment and refreshment to fuel you along the way. What you do in one stage either helps you or hurts you in later stages. You need the drive to carry forward despite the inevitable pain and hardship. You need fans. And you need to take personal accountability for your career success. Careers are a combination of skill, planning, and luck.[5] You need the skill and the planning to make you eligible for the luck.

---

5   See Richard Feloni, "20 People Who Became Highly Successful After Age 40," *Business Insider*, September 9, 2014, www.businessinsider.com/people-who-became-successful-after-age-40-2014-9?IR=T6.

CHAPTER 5

Career Inventory and Ecosystem

The purpose of the Career Inventory is to help you take stock of the major career assets that you currently have onboard. Think about the three major types of fuel for your career:

- Transportable Skills
- Meaningful Experiences
- Enduring Relationships

For a downloadable copy of the Career Inventory and all other exercises in this book, visit **thelongviewcareer.com**

Fuel #1: Transportable Skills

Transportable skills are the capabilities you've acquired that you can carry with you from job to job, company to company, and industry to industry over the course of your career. List them.

Academic degrees, professional credentials

_____

_____

_____

Languages, including music and computer languages

_____

_____

_____

Name the strengths that are frequently mentioned by bosses and peers and in your 360-degree and performance evaluations.

_____

_____

_____

What feedback have you received on your emotional intelligence (aka EQ)—do bosses and colleagues comment on your ability to read social situations and communicate emotionally?

_____

_____

_____

Your Talent Ledger. Think of the people you have hired and/or promoted so far in your career. Did they rise and grow in their careers? Would the best ones want to work for you again?

_____

_____

_____

Fuel #2: Meaningful Experiences

Write down some of the meaningful experiences you have had—inside and outside of work—that might help demonstrate the diversity of your life and career to date.

Personal travel

_____

_____

_____

International work assignments

_____

_____

_____

Worked in a large corporate environment

_____

_____

_____

Entrepreneurship/start-up experience

_____

_____

_____

Community/volunteer activities

_____

_____

_____

Major events, product launches, famous initiatives to which you personally contributed

_____

_____

_____

Public speaking/writing/performance experiences

_____

_____

_____

Teaching/advisory/mentoring experiences

_____

_____

_____

Hobbies, activities, and passions outside of work

_____

_____

_____

Other life experiences and challenges

_____

_____

_____

Fuel #3: Enduring Relationships aka Your Career Ecosystem

"No one—not rock stars, not professional athletes, not software billionaires, and not even geniuses—ever makes it alone." —Malcolm Gladwell in *Outliers*

Over time, each of us becomes surrounded by an ecosystem made up of the key people and communities who strongly influence our career destinies. I encourage people to periodically take stock of their career ecosystem and make sure that they are creating the right kind of support around them. There are many layers to a career ecosystem, and they extend far beyond your current job and employer.

1. **Contacts** are the raw, unrefined ingredients for the ecosystem—the LinkedIn contacts, e-mail addresses, alumni association members, coworkers, etc. who enter our lives. Periodically, size up your own collection of career connections. Are you making new connections? Are you keeping the database fresh and up-to-date? Are you benignly losing touch with people in your network that you respect?

What is the approximate number of contacts you have in each of the below platforms?

- LinkedIn Contacts
- Facebook Friends
- Twitter Followers
- Instagram Followers
- Personal e-mail directory
- Other social platforms/networks

Alumni associations you belong to (schools/past employers, etc.)

_____

_____

_____

Other membership groups or industry associations

_____

_____

_____

Any other major contacts that might have impact on your career—today or someday

_____

_____

_____

A lot of people incorrectly think "It's all about contacts," as though that's where career success begins and ends. Raw connections are useful to extend your reach, but they aren't of significant value until you convert them to a higher relationship—those people who will engage and mobilize on your behalf. You may end up with thousands of raw connections. But remember, it is not just a volume game; it is about quality and impact.

Ben Casnocha, the coauthor of *The Start-up of You* along with LinkedIn founder Reid Hoffman, underscores this point clearly. "There's a distinction between networking and genuine relationship building. Networkers are transactional. They pursue relationships thinking only about what other people can do for them. Relationship builders, on the other hand, try to help other people first. They don't keep score. They're aware that most good deeds get reciprocated, but they're not calculated about it. And they think about their relationships all the time, not just when they need something."

2. A Community of Experts is a higher level in the ecosystem. These are the people who have special knowledge and access that can help you succeed in your job and in your career. They bring subject matter expertise and best practices to your solutions, and that makes you better and smarter. This community needs to be recruited and nurtured, but the best way is not just by asking for help, but by offering it. Some of this community will be found in your immediate circle of work colleagues, but some can come from further afield.

Who is in your community of experts? Which topic areas are covered, and where do you need more help? Are you holding up your side of the bargain by responding to their requests with good input? If you were to move companies or cities, who might you lose from your community, and how would you fill the void?

When you are faced with a problem you don't know the answer to, what are some of the expert sources that you consult? (These experts can be sources like Google, specific blogs, or individual experts. And often we use different "experts" for different types of problems.)

Expert Source	I consult them for...

In my own work, I get hit with tough questions every week that I cannot possibly know the answers to. But I have a wide enough community of experts inside and outside our firm that I can answer almost anything within twenty-four hours. Over the past three decades, I have accumulated a list in my head (and in my e-mail directory) of about a hundred true experts who are able and willing to help me solve problems in various areas of expertise. Maybe one third of them work in my current company. The others are people I have connected with over the years and have probably exchanged some knowledge with. It is a pleasure when I discover a new expert, and I work hard to respond to their requests with some urgency. It's easy to forget some of the terrific experts we know. In the past year, I have probably discovered ten exceptional new experts through referrals from other experts, or just by working directly with them on projects. A few in my expert community have faded away because they were chronically unresponsive, or haven't stayed current on their subject. I take a look at my e-mail directory and LinkedIn connections at least once a year to remind me of the expertise that is often just a click or call away.

3. Critical Colleagues are the five to ten people in your current company who decisively influence your progress. The list starts with your boss, who is consistently rated in research as the number one influence on job success and happiness. Your boss's boss is also a critical influencer. If your immediate supervisor proposes you for a raise or promotion, their boss almost always needs to endorse and approve it. So if your boss's boss thinks you are a genius (or an idiot!) it makes a big difference to your pathway. Certain peers and subordinates are also in your sphere of critical colleagues. As you contemplate your career ecosystem, think about these ten or so golden relationships in your current organization. Candidly, what do they think of you? Would they support you in a move forward? If not, what do you need to do to correct a misperception or to earn a better relationship?

Critical Colleague	State of Relationship (Positive/Neutral/Negative)

4. Champions are the mentors and advocates who help advise, support, and propel you in your career. This is usually a very small number of people—often five or fewer. These are the kinds of people you will meet in your "career heaven." Champions are like a fifteen-mile-per-hour tailwind for our careers, a benevolent hidden hand that propels us forward. Champions say good things about you behind your back, and promote your cause to others.

> Name the people you believe are—or could become—your champions. (If you're stuck, think of who recommended you for your college, or who supported you for a job or promotion.)

> _____

> _____

> _____

Katya Andresen, the CEO of Cricket Media, defines the three principal roles that mentors can play in our lives: the Star, a successful role model who shows us how it can be done, the Sage, who like Socrates doesn't give us the answer but teaches us how to think, and the Agitator, who spurs us and stretches us, and gives us the occasional kick in the pants.

We accumulate these champions over the course of our lives. People ask me: "Where do I find them, and how do I sign them up?" The best approach is to be patient and open, and when you discover a champion, appreciate and nurture the mentorship. They often don't need heavy maintenance. Mentors just love to hear how you are doing, and to share a little bit in your successes and struggles. As Katya says,

"If you put yourself in the mind of a student, you will find teachers. When you find someone who sparks your career, do all you can to work for them, be useful to them, or spend time with them. If you are lucky enough to get their ear and their guidance, be a sponge. Great mentors like to see someone throwing their heart, mind, and soul into learning. Build a relationship by being a good student and a hard worker. Be loyal and committed to them and what they are trying to accomplish. And above all, be appreciative. Show them the impact they made, and thank them early and often. Also, consider serving as a mentor—either as a volunteer at a nonprofit or for a colleague or student aspiring to advance in your field. Being someone's star, sage, or agitator is a wonderful way to honor those who were there for you and to discover the deepest of joys: making a real difference for someone else."

Some people think of the champions in their career ecosystem like their personal "board." Alvaro Saralegui rose up through the ranks at Time Inc. and is an advisor to the National Football League. Alvaro says: "Make sure your mentors aren't just about the wisdom of the past. Find champions who are part of your past, your present *and* your future."

Once you discover a mentor or champion, the main thing is to appreciate them, and to stay engaged with them. Periodically send them a note to let them know how you're doing. Share victories and failures. Ask advice. Remember, to your mentor, this kind of communication isn't a burden. It is a reward. Who are the mentors in your career today? Who might become your next one? Are you doing enough to nurture and earn their support?

Map out your career ecosystem at least once per year. Write down the key relationships you have earned across all four layers—connections, community of experts, critical colleagues, and champions. Which relationships are bringing you the most value in your professional career? Which ones are withering away? Which ones offer you the best opportunities to give and to grow? Were there any surprises? Are there any areas that are lacking, or relationships that are underdeveloped? The key to managing these relationships is to do it with intention, and not just blindly reach out to hundreds of people.

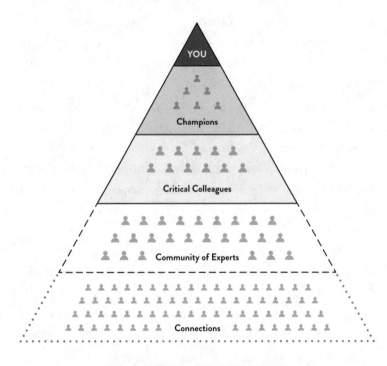

CAREER ECOSYSTEM

5. You. The center of any career ecosystem is you. It is obvious to many, but completely true. You are the brand manager of you. One of your jobs as brand manager is to keep an eye on your career ecosystem and make sure it is positive and fresh. One millennial rising star I know does an annual "energy audit" on the people affecting her career. She finds that some people in her sphere—even if they are good personal friends, well-intentioned, and very supportive in the past—now seem to bring her down and hold her back. They will be the first to say "That can't be done," or, "You shouldn't even try to do that." She will try to spend more time with other people in her ecosystem, those individuals who make her feel bigger, smarter, and more energized.

Annual Career Value Size-Up

About once per year, set goals for the year ahead, and take a look back at the year past. There are four great questions to ask:

1. Am I learning and growing?
2. Am I having an impact on individuals, the organization, and even society at large?
3. Am I having fun?
4. Am I being appropriately rewarded and building economic value?

You can assign equal importance to these four factors, or weight them according to your personal ambition for the year ahead. At some stages of your career, Learning might be very highly weighted and Rewards a bit less. In other stages, you might really be looking for Impact and Fun, and other factors might be less relevant. At some times, money might be really important to you, and Rewards will be weighted more heavily. Assign a percentage weighting to each factor so that they add up to 100 percent.

At the end of the year, spend a day reflecting on your contributions, progress, and outcomes from the past twelve months.

Give yourself a rating out of ten for each question. When it comes to Learning, what new transportable skills, meaningful experiences, and enduring relationships have you added? As you consider Impact, think about the benefits that the work you do brings to customers, coworkers, the organization and society in general. Fun will be a very personal assessment. Is work a joyful place for you or a den of dread? On Rewards, remember to look not only at base salary, but at the full picture including base salary, benefits, pensions, vacation, personal days/flex time, expenses paid or subsidized by your employer, plus any changes in the ownership or equity you may be accumulating.

It will be interesting to look at your weightings, self-ratings, and total Career Value scores over time. Since these are very personal evaluations, it is hard to develop quantitative benchmarks. In my experience, any score over 700 is very good—you are generally satisfied with the things that are important to you. Any score below 500 should prompt some serious consideration: Am I looking for the right things? Are my expectations right? Is this the right job for me? Do not obsess over the math. What's important is that you periodically take stock of the big drivers of your career, and make constructive changes.

Annual Career Value—Example 1

Here is an example for someone in Stage One of their career who equally values the four questions (each receives a 25 percent weighting) and who gives themselves satisfaction scores between nine and six across the four areas.

Goal Area	Weighting	Your self-assessment out of 10	Career Value
Learning	25%	9	225
Impact	25%	7	175
Fun	25%	6	150
Reward	25%	6	150
TOTAL ANNUAL CAREER VALUE			**700**

When you multiply out the weightings and scores, this individual achieved an Annual Career Value Score of 700—which is very healthy. The score of nine on Learning is extremely promising, as they clearly feel they are building skills for the future. The Fun quotient is a bit low and needs some attention. Are there activities inside and outside of work that can build more joy into this person's work life—i.e. joining a club at work, adding a fresh new assignment, improving work-life balance? On the Rewards front, this person should look hard at their contributions over the past year, and get some competitive benchmarks. Are they unhappy because they are truly underrewarded, or because their expectations are out of line? Talk to their company about what the rewards pathway might be, and what can be done to accelerate it. This person should not make a knee-jerk move to find a better paying job that promises to be more fun. They should be very cautious about leaving a job where they are getting good scores on Learning and Impact. Those are really hard to replicate.

Annual Career Value—Example 2

Here is an individual in Stage One with identical scores, but who has a different weighting of the four questions.

Goal Area	Weighting	Your self-assessment out of 10	Career Value
Learning	60%	9	540
Impact	10%	7	70
Fun	10%	6	60
Reward	20%	6	120
TOTAL ANNUAL CAREER VALUE			**790**

This individual receives an Annual Career Value score ninety points higher, mainly because they see themselves as doing well on the thing that they value most—Learning. For this individual, the key strategy is to keep learning—seeking out assignments and bosses that will continue to build their learning curve. As their career progresses, they may want to adjust the weightings they assign to the four questions, in which case they will need more balanced scores in order to stay well satisfied with their career.

Annual Career Value—Example 3

This example reflects an individual in Stage Two who is aggressively looking to build economic wealth, hence the 60 percent weighting on Rewards. They are willing to place less emphasis (at least for this year or so) on Learning, Impact, and Fun in order to max out on financial returns. This is fine as long as the rewards are actually delivered, and the individual is willing to make the trade-offs on other factors.

Goal Area	Weighting	Your self-assessment out of 10	Career Value
Learning	20%	5	100
Impact	10%	3	30
Fun	10%	4	40
Reward	60%	9	540
TOTAL ANNUAL CAREER VALUE			**710**

The individual in this example ended up with a very good Annual Career Value score of 710, but only because the money met their expectations. What would have happened if the money had fallen short? If the Rewards score had only been five, the total score would have fallen to 470. Someone who is very oriented toward Rewards needs to make sure that: 1) they are in a career environment where exceptional performance is systematically rewarded; 2) they are absolutely clear on the criteria for success and are confident that they can achieve their expectations; 3) they do not allow the other factors to stagnate for too long. In my experience, at some point the pursuit of money alone becomes boring and limiting. Review your goals and weightings very carefully throughout your career. The weightings can and should change from year to year. Do not allow money to determine your whole view of career satisfaction. Always leave room for Learning, Impact and Fun.

Annual Career Value—Example 4

Example four reflects someone in Stage Three who is primarily seeking Impact. This individual has retired from

full-time employment and is seeking a career phase where
they can give and contribute in a meaningful way. Fun and
Learning are secondary, and Rewards are only of marginal
importance to this individual.

Goal Area	Weighting	Your self-assessment out of 10	Career Value
Learning	20%	7	140
Impact	50%	9	450
Fun	20%	7	140
Reward	10%	3	30
TOTAL ANNUAL CAREER VALUE			**760**

Based on the self-assessment scores, the total Annual
Career Value is 760, suggesting that the strategy is working
extremely well. The monetary rewards are paltry, but that
is not important to this individual at this stage of their
career. This person is experiencing the Impact they crave,
with healthy doses of Learning and Fun. If Rewards were
to become very important, this career path would not be
not sustainable. But it is a great place for someone seeking
Impact above all else.

CHAPTER 6

Your Personal Time Portfolio

"Time is the coin of your life. It is the only coin
you have, and only you can determine how
it will be spent." —Carl Sandburg

If you ask a skilled financial advisor how to get the best yield out your investments over the long haul, they'll tell you that "asset allocation" is the key. That is, are you investing in the right kinds of things at the right time—stocks, bonds, commodities, and other asset classes? The same is true of careers, but the key variable is how you invest your *time*. By looking at how we actually invest our time, we learn where we are placing emphasis, and what seems to be yielding the outcomes we are looking for. Our time portfolios reveal where we can make trade-offs that could make us happier and more successful.

The pie charts shown below are based on real examples

for myself and other executives I know. They show the approximate percentage of time devoted to various activities. Conveniently, there are about a hundred waking hours in the average week, so it's easy for you to do this exercise, too. I classified my hundred hours into broad categories like Work, Family, Health & Wellness, Teaching & Learning, and Community. It's not critical that you use exactly the same categories or that you have precise hourly estimates. Do it for yourself and a few people you know, and you'll get the point. This first pie chart is illustrative of me in my early thirties in the midst of Stage One. I was an up-and-coming executive at Ogilvy Canada. I was married, with two young children.

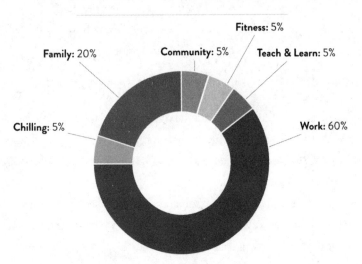

MY PERSONAL TIME PORTFOLIO: 30'S

Fitness: 5%

Family: 20%   Community: 5%   Teach & Learn: 5%

Chilling: 5%   Work: 60%

Work is at 60 percent. Like lots of my peers, I worked hard. I could do eighty hours a week for a short burst if I absolutely needed to, but found that I maxed out at sixty hours per week on a sustained basis.

Family is at about 20 percent. This included a few hours a day with the kids at bedtime and some family activities on the weekend. Not exactly Dad-of-the-Year stuff, but Child Services was never called!

Chilling is at 5 percent. The occasional dinner out and some weekly zombie time, usually in front of the TV.

Community is at 5 percent. Minimal volunteer service. I started to get involved with a local charity: Goodwill Industries.

Fitness is at 5 percent. In my thirties I joined a gym and reactivated my beer-league hockey career.

Teaching and Learning is at maybe 5 percent. I did a few industry lectures a year, plus some training at work.

For contrast, this second chart is my time portfolio now that I am in my fifties.

MY PERSONAL TIME PORTFOLIO: 50'S

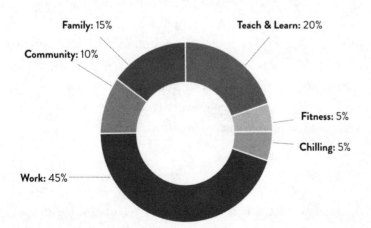

Family: 15%   Teach & Learn: 20%

Community: 10%

Fitness: 5%

Chilling: 5%

Work: 45%

Working in a traditional sense is now down to 45 percent, but as discussed below I have re-invested a lot of my work time into teaching and advisory activities. So I still put in about sixty hours a week, but the nature of the work is quite different

Family time is down a touch to 15 percent, as my wife and I are now empty nesters. Family time is now often focused around travel together.

Chilling is steady at 5 percent. I still need my downtime and zombie time. In addition to time socializing with friends, my chilling time now includes playing guitar—often while watching really bad television.

Fitness is steady at 5 percent. A few trips to the gym and Sunday night hockey are a critical part of my weekly balance.

Community plays a bigger role in my fifties than before, increasing to 10 percent. There are a few organizations where I like the people and the mission, and feel I can contribute in some meaningful way. I find this kind of community work is an excellent source of energy.

Teaching and Learning time has seen the big change as training, mentoring, lecturing, and a range of industry and advisory board roles now take up around 20 percent of my time. It also includes an active learning component, which is an important dimension. For me, every Saturday morning begins at 8:30 a.m. with a guitar lesson. It's hard to think of work when you are playing Hendrix.

Below is a time portfolio for a very talented colleague of mine from when he was in his thirties. He worked incredibly hard—not just occasionally, but all the time. He barely had time for his young family. He tried to meet with friends, but often had to cancel "because I'm too busy with work." He let his hobbies lapse, again citing work reasons. This executive burned out at forty, was unemployed for almost two years, and suffered a near breakdown. I believe that the lack of diversity in his time portfolio was a clear contributing factor. All work all the time is a recipe for burnout. It's like a severely monotonous diet. I really like chicken. But eating only chicken all the time would make me very tired and angry. The same is true of work. At least some change of pace is needed for inspiration and refreshment.

TIME PORTFOLIO OF A BURNOUT

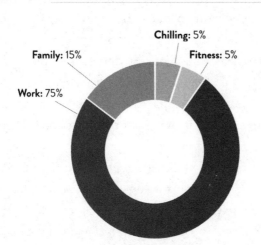

It's quite illuminating to estimate your personal time portfolio at least once a year. Which of your investments of time seem to be yielding the most encouraging results? Is your allocation of time changing? Are there some reallocations you would like to test out for three or six months?

There is no magic percentage formula, and no ideal time portfolio. That's why it's called "personal." We all have different tolerances for work and stress, and varying appetites for community, work, and even family. But having done this personal time portfolio exercise for myself and at least a hundred other people, I have a few observations and suggestions to share.

A lot of people focus on the Work slice of the pie. That's a good place to start because it's pretty clear that working hard is still a key. According to Gallup research, the percentage of people working sixty or more hours per week has increased from 9 to 17 percent over the past decade.[6] But many of the most interesting dynamics happen in the other slices. Activities like Teaching & Learning and Community seem to have a disproportionate impact on happiness and success. This is consistent with what Adam Grant wrote about in *Give and Take*—learning, giving advice, and helping others can have profound effects on our energy levels and impact. I look at these activities as the vitamins and nutrients of a successful career. They provide nourishment and freshness. They make you better at work.

It is hard to make the pie bigger, so we have to make tough trade-offs. Much has been written on the harmful effects of sustained lack of sleep—science strongly suggests that cheating ourselves out of sleep is a losing proposition. Some people think instead that multi-tasking is the magic answer. I believe that you can sometimes multi-task when both tasks are mundane—like folding laundry and watching a rerun on TV. But when you really look at outcomes, not

---

6   See Gallup.com.

just activity levels, the truth is most of us are lousy at multi-tasking. We might be busier, but we are not more effective. When we must make the hard trade-offs in our time portfolios and cut back on something, I urge you not to cut out one of your non-Work priorities completely. Cut it back, but try your best not to lose it completely. We are creatures of habit, and when a habit goes to zero, it is so much harder to build it back up. Even small portions of the high-potency ingredients like teaching, community work, and fitness can make a huge difference.

One of the biggest sources of stress is the collision between work and family. Chapter 11 goes into the topic in much more detail, but here's a tactic that I have used hundreds of times. For the past twenty or more years, I have traveled extensively for business, often spending over 150 days per year on the road. I have developed an approach I call "proactive time shifting," and here is how it works. My daughter Alison's September birthday collides pretty much every year with a chronically heavy period of work and travel for me. So I do some proactive time shifting that goes something like this.

"Hi Alison."

"Yes, Dad." (Often this is accompanied by pronounced eye rolling.)

"Your birthday is coming up soon."

"Yes, Dad. Just like every year."

"Well, I am going to be in Tokyo at that time on business, and there's a huge chance that I would have to fly through the night to get home for your birthday, or I'd just plain miss it completely. So, how about if we shift your birthday celebration to another weekend of your choice when I'm back from Japan? You choose the date and how you want to celebrate, and I'll be there."

Between us, Alison and I have time-shifted probably three quarters of her twenty-five birthdays, and I don't think I have totally missed a single one. The first point about proactive time shifting is that it must actually be proactive. Note that I had the conversation with Alison in July or August, not from some airport lounge or conference room in Tokyo the day before her birthday. And it was definitely two-way—Alison made some choices and worked out the probabilities with me. Look ahead in your calendar for potential collisions and danger zones. Have grown-up conversations about options and probabilities, especially with kids.

Aside from proactive time shifting, many of the successful people I talk to refer to boundaries and mindfulness as coping strategies in a hectic career. I used to think that I could enjoy so-called family time while simultaneously plowing through work e-mail. I can't. I need harder edges. It is better for me to work with intensity in short bursts than to drift between work and family modes. The same is true for me on vacation. I cannot ever really get 100 percent off the work grid for sustained periods, but I do work hard to compartmentalize the work intrusions into well-known slots. It is much better for me to set aside, say, 6:30 a.m. to 8:30 a.m. on Tuesday and Thursday during a vacation week than to live under the cloud of a work-related lightning strike at any moment.

• • •

Community work and volunteer activities can be highly energizing, even in small doses. People often say, "I'll start doing volunteer work when I'm retired." In my opinion, you cannot start too early. I am always impressed by busy young people who somehow carve out an hour or two from their schedules to volunteer. I started working with Goodwill Industries as a volunteer "marketing advisor" when I was still in my twenties. I am still involved with the organization today as a board member. Along the way, I learned skills that still pay dividends decades later.

The evidence is overwhelming that even a small regular investment in Fitness & Wellness time pays big dividends. (See Tom Rath's excellent book *Are You Fully Charged?*) It's not that more time at the gym always equates to more success, but it is clear that individuals need to invest in fitness at least to some threshold level. Creating a regular habit is critical, ideally a daily one. When we are busy or tired, we tend to eliminate fitness time, just at the moment we need it most. Whether it's yoga, hockey, spinning class, or running—making it a regular part of your life adds voltage to your career.

One of the places you can often uncover wasted hours to reinvest is your commute to work. The average commute to and from work in major US cities is almost two hours. For some, it just seems like wasted time, or a chance to bone up on their road rage. My colleague Dimitri Maex has a high-stress job as president of our number one OgilvyOne office worldwide, along with a full family life and a budding side job as a DJ and composer. Dimitri commutes to work on a bicycle, and turns two hours of New York City traffic hell into a daily fitness workout. Some people convert their train commutes into highly productive time for reading and writing. Others walk to work while listening to educational podcasts or audiobooks. What a great way to learn a new language, explore new trends in your industry, or develop a new career skill. When I drive into work early in the morning, I use the time for calls with Asia and Europe because the time zones work out so conveniently. At the end of the day, I talk to the West Coast, or call my mother in Canada. Commuting time can be a waste or a pain. How could you invest your commuting time for higher joy and higher yield? Are there other pockets of time you could be using?

CHAPTER 7

Career Path Navigator

"When your values are clear to you, making
decisions becomes easier." —Roy E. Disney

"The key to making healthy decisions is to
respect your future self." —A.J. Jacobs

All along our career paths, we will face decision points and
crossroads:

"Should I stay or should I go?"

"Is it time for an MBA or some other postgraduate
degree?"

"I've just been proposed for a transfer in my company.
Should I take it?"

"Is it time to reboot my career and try something
dramatically different?"

"I just got passed over (or fired). Now what?"

Everyone struggles with how to make the right call. In my view, too many people make arbitrary and relatively short-term decisions about their careers. It's pretty easy to do a superficial side-by-side comparison of two jobs and check off the obvious pros and cons. Will I get more pay? Does it come with a sexier title, or more vacation, or a better dental plan?

These kinds of technical comparisons miss the point. You need to put your choices into a bigger context. I've put the Career Path Navigator at the end of this section on tools because I think you need to do some of the other groundwork first. Do some career math to get in the right frame of mind. Think about the three big stages to remind yourself where you are in your long career journey. Do a career inventory and size up your current career ecosystem to take stock of where you stand with your skills and relationships. Contemplate your time portfolio and see what kind of balance seems to make sense in your career and life. Now you're ready to make some enlightened decisions.

Throughout our careers, we are seeking our sweet spot—the intersection between what we are good at, what we love to do, and what the world will appreciate. We never get it right the first time. I tell people it is like trying to land a helicopter on an aircraft carrier at sea. The seas are roiling. The winds are howling. The deck of the ship is pitching. But somehow we need to land ourselves safely in the right zone.

Our career choices along the way help us explore, define, and home in on our sweet spot. I've used the Career Path Navigator hundreds of time to help people think about their options. It starts with three questions.

First, what is your career ambition, or at least a hypothesis

CAREER PATH NAVIGATOR

Your Career Ambition:

"To become _____ within _____ years."

Fuel you currently have:	Fuel you need to get there:
1. _____	1. _____
2. _____	2. _____
3. _____	3. _____
4. _____	4. _____
5. _____	5. _____

CAREER PATHWAY A

Role / Job: _____

Fuel you will

acquire here: _____

CAREER PATHWAY B

Role / Job: _____

Fuel you will

acquire here: _____

CAREER PATHWAY C

Role / Job: _____

Fuel you will

acquire here: _____

CAREER PATHWAY D

Role / Job: _____

Fuel you will

acquire here: _____

Which pathway(s) get you the fuel you
need to achieve your ambition?

on where you might want to go? Next, what "fuel" do you currently have on board? And finally, what fuel do you need to achieve your ultimate ambition? This encourages people to think not just about the nuts and bolts of job choices, but about the pathway, and whether this specific decision will open or close more doors for you down the road. "Given where I am today, and where I'd like to go, which option gives me the greatest chance of getting to my destination?"

Jamie is a rising star in a large communications firm. He is a highly effective thinker and doer. His firm loves him and has given him a mountain of work and copious amounts of exposure to different tasks. Like most people in their twenties, Jamie doesn't exactly know what he wants to do long-term, but when pressed over a beer, he volunteers, "Someday, I'd like to become an office leader."

As Jamie thinks about what it takes, and where he has gaps, he concludes that his current task load is fine, but it won't actually lead him to the promised land. He definitely needs to learn how to manage a profit and loss statement and drive a business. Jamie needs to build up his "talent magnetism" so that he will be not just a doer but also a leader of others. If he wants to run an international office, he will need to prove that he can work with global clients, not just local ones. And in the years ahead, he must build relationships with more senior executives and the head of global HR in his firm, because he is not currently being considered for office leadership jobs. Now, Jamie can look at job options in this light and make some intelligent choices over the next several years. He's not just wondering what a good job is, he is also thinking about which assignments are richest in these development factors. I checked in with

Jamie. He has found a great assignment within his current firm that will develop these needed skills and is now on an excellent leadership pathway.

While some people, like Jamie, are looking to increase their leadership profile, others are looking to further their education. A lot of people ask me about postgraduate degrees. I do not have one and have never really regretted it. I always felt that my work experience at "teaching hospitals" like Procter & Gamble and Ogilvy & Mather gave me most of what I'd learn getting an MBA. These companies were very focused on training, and I was always very focused on learning. I checked the LinkedIn profiles of twenty of the most successful CEOs I know personally. Just over half of them have MBAs.

In some fields and for some individuals, there is no question that a postgraduate degree can often add extra value. The reasons to do a Masters degree are very personal. You need to decide what special value it will bring to your career. Will it:

- Add transportable skills you do not currently possess?
- Help you re-invent yourself and change the vector of your career?
- Establish new personal connections and expand your career ecosystem?
- Add an important credential that you do not currently have?

- Accelerate your process of discovery—to test a hypothesis about what you're actually good at and love to do?

One Masters program definitely focused on the development side is the Sloan Fellows MBA from the MIT Sloan School of Management. The MIT Sloan Fellows pursue a full-time immersive twelve-month program designed for mid-career professionals. Students tend to be in their thirties, and 75 percent are from outside the USA. Stephen Sacca, director of the program, describes it as "a leadership program that happens to confer an MBA. It is not really for people who want to totally redirect their careers or get a credential. It is for people who are successful in their current jobs but feel they can do more to change their industries." One of the current MIT Sloan Fellows is a classical opera singer who feels that the music business needs some serious business disruption in order to survive. She is using her MIT Sloan Fellows experience to build the business skills and global network that will help her take on the challenge.

The ROI of an MBA

For many years, the notion that an MBA would pay for itself over time was a foregone conclusion. It is not so obvious these days. Some people seek a concrete financial return on investment. If you want to do the math for yourself, think about the cost of MBA itself—i.e. the tuition fees, books, and supplies, plus perhaps incremental travel, living and housing costs, plus possible student loan interest. If you are leaving work to study, add the opportunity cost of not earning a salary for one or two years. This could easily total $200,000 in after-tax total costs. Ask yourself, "Is it reasonable to expect I'll earn an extra $200,000 in after-tax earnings over the course of my career?" Remembering how long a career can last, this might be a very reasonable expectation for some people. If the math doesn't work, don't give up on the thought of a Masters. Just make sure you are doing it for compelling personal reasons.

One of the most interesting and epic career decisions I observed in recent years involves Mohammed Ashour. Let's meet Mohammed.

Profile: Medical School or Cricket Ranching?

MOHAMMED ASHOUR
Age 28

Role	CEO of Aspire
Sweet Spot	The intersection of medicine, business and purpose

"For the first time in my life, the idea of not going back to medicine has become a possibility." Considering he'd always dreamed of becoming a neurosurgeon, Mohammed Ashour knows this sounds crazy. When he goes on to describe his new venture, it starts to sound even crazier. Mohammed is building Aspire, a multi-national company that produces insects for food. "It's the work I was born to do," he explains.

Mohammed, twenty-eight, is used to the reactions of surprise and confusion when he tells people about Aspire, the company he cofounded one semester into his joint MD-MBA degree at McGill University. The idea was born as a submission to the prestigious Hult Prize, an annual award governed by the Clinton Global Initiative and the Hult International Business School. Each year the Hult Prize challenges business schools to come up with venture ideas on how to improve the world, and in 2013 the brief was to tackle food security and help feed the world's poor. Over 10,000 teams participated for the chance to win $1 million of funding for the winning proposal.

The McGill team came up with a startling and powerful concept: breed and market insects—mainly crickets, grasshoppers and weevils—for human consumption. According to their research, insects are a tremendous source of protein that consume far fewer resources to produce compared to alternatives like beef and chicken. Furthermore, millions of people around the world, primarily in Africa and South America, already consume insects as a part of their diet. The main challenge would be how to secure the food supply chain and ensure that demand for these insects could be fulfilled reliably, cost effectively, and with high quality control.

Mohammed's team won the regional competition and advanced to the finals in New York City. There, in front of an audience that included former President Bill Clinton, they claimed the top prize of $1 million. For Mohammed, the win created a thorny dilemma. "I knew I was leaving big money on the table by not going into healthcare management at that moment. I had my MBA studies under my belt and a ton of employer interest after the Clinton-Hult Prize win. I had a new baby back at home, and people were sticking crazy offers in front of me." He had to decide between going back to school to complete the medical school portion of his dual degree, accepting one of the many lucrative employment opportunities, or focusing on running Aspire full time. "I had to choose one path, and if I chose Aspire there was a risk that it would fail," he said. "And there was also a risk that I would never finish my medical degree. I had dreamed of being a doctor since I was eight years old, and the thought of never realizing that goal was pretty daunting."

To complicate matters further, Mohammed had to contend with the skepticism he encountered from his family, who were well-intentioned but worried about the stability he would be giving up to pursue an unconventional dream. He had already spent years working toward becoming a doctor: he held a Bachelor of Science degree in psychology and biology from the University of Toronto and a Masters in neuroscience from McGill University. "I did not grow up in an entrepreneurial family. We have a lot of professionals—engineers, doctors and bankers—but no entrepreneurs. They didn't understand how I could give up a set path in favor of the unknown."

For Mohammed, it came down to the reasons he had decided to pursue medicine in the first place: the opportunity to create a noble legacy, the desire to have a positive impact, and the ability to be financially stable. At Aspire, he would be able to do all of those things—and possibly at a greater magnitude—just not in the way he had always envisioned.

In the end, he decided to put med school on hold and focus on building Aspire full time. He moved with his young family to Austin, Texas, where Aspire has since set up an insect breeding facility. The company survived its first two years of operations and the team has grown to sixteen staff. Things look promising, though Mohammed knows there are no guarantees. "I know I could do something that was a more obvious pathway for me like working on Wall Street or in medicine. But for now, nothing can offer me the growth and impact and satisfaction of trying to start a social enterprise with a great team. It may not work, but I will never regret trying."

Mohammed's chosen pathway wasn't the easiest one or the most popular one. But it was a smart bet given his long-term goals. Only time will tell if it was ultimately the right answer. He put it in context and thought through the angles. He made a decision and stuck to it.

Author and angel investor Auren Hoffman has some great advice for people who are focused on the long term and looking for serious growth. He is mainly talking about choosing between start-ups, but his wisdom could work for anyone who is seeking hyper-growth and willing to take the risk and consequences.

According to Auren, "Long-term success requires massive growth. Most smart people out of college grow an average of 10 percent per year. Which means they are roughly twice as effective seven years after graduating college. That makes sense, as most twenty-nine-year-olds make double what they did their first job out of college. To grow even more quickly, you need a job with the following criteria:

- You're surrounded by people who are smarter than you
- You have an opportunity to fail
- The company has a history of giving massive responsibility to people like you

Auren says, "Find a company where at least 30 percent of the people are smarter than you, as you will grow the most through the people who surround you, so those people need to be really impressive. Because people tend to hire those they know, many of these people will likely be your colleagues for the next thirty years. So pick your colleagues wisely. One simple heuristic to determine how smart the people are at the company are is how selective they are in hiring. You want to pick a company that has a really hard (and often long) recruiting process where you need to meet a lot of people, complete a project, and have some grueling interviews. While not perfect, at least you know that everyone else the company hired went through the same process."

Hoffman continues: "You grow the most when you have a 33 to 66 percent chance of failure. To improve, you want to be in a position where success is not guaranteed. Too often, people (especially recent grads) are put into jobs that they will definitely succeed at. And while definite success initially feels good, it doesn't help you grow. You should find an organization that will give you projects where there is a high chance of failure.

"Assuming you are an ambitious person who wants to have continued growth, you want the opportunity to be promoted and to be given continuously greater responsibility. The companies that are most likely to promote you quickly have a history of doing so and are experiencing high growth. Find people that joined the company with a similar profile as you and see if some of these people were given outsized responsibility in the company."

Whether you are look at a start-up or other options, career decisions are chock-full of emotions and the frailties of human psychology. Chris Graves is Global Chairman of Ogilvy Public Relations and a noted expert on behavioral economics. Chris alerts us to beware of the natural human biases that creep into our decision-making, including those around our careers.

"We constantly undervalue benefits that come in the future. It's a phenomenon called 'temporal discounting.' We all resist taking on pain in the present (harder work, less salary, less prestige) in order to gain something in the future—even if the future benefit will actually end up greater. As humans, we just don't trust that the future benefits will come, and we factor them down very sharply." Chris also observes how "loss aversion" comes into play. "People see the consequences and risks more clearly than the upside. We dream vaguely but dread precisely."

Knowing about your possible biases towards the present and away from risk is important. It is also critically important to make career decisions in the right frame of mind. Don't be bullied by a boss or headhunter to make a snap decision. Daniel Kahneman's book *Thinking, Fast and Slow* describes an exhaustive collection of experiments demonstrating how often people come to conclusions confidently and wrongly. One of the destructive behaviors I have seen in recent years is what I call the "career flash mob." One member in a group of friends gets a new job and sends out a text or Facebook post after about a week that says something like: "Life here at Startup Wizard totally rocks. Best job ever. They're hiring. I'm lonely. Come check it out." The message creates a frenzy of immediate job applications from the circle of friends, and within two months at least half of them are working at Startup Wizard. Until they discover that it doesn't actually rock at all, and someone moves on to Startup Genius and creates a whole new cycle. Discovery is good. Pointless change is not.

Don't entrust your career to flash mobs or any other knee-jerk urge to change. Talk to at least three people in your current firm before making a decision (your boss, HR, and at least one other trusted voice in the organization). You owe it to yourself to explore options in your current company. Often there is important new information that could sway your decision. Recently, a talented young woman left our firm to work for a competitor. She loved our culture but assumed she could only get the kind of experience she was seeking outside our company. A few days before her fait accompli resignation, our company had agreed to open a new division that would be perfectly aligned with her ambitions. Because she didn't test her assumptions before she signed up for the new job, both she and the company missed an opportunity. It is healthy and constructive to express your ambitions to your bosses. But your goal should be about creating a pathway and a timetable, not necessarily an instant solution. If you deliver an ultimatum with only a few days for the company to respond, you need to be prepared for the consequences. Most of the time, the company will not make a counter offer. It is also worth reading the thoughtful article from the Wharton School at the University of Pennsylvania called "The Grass is Not Always Greener."

So your job is to take stock of your ambitions, skills, and options, and make absolutely sure you are operating on the correct assumptions about your current situation. Think about the assignment and the learning curve more than the title. Be prepared to stretch yourself and take risks. It's okay to be scared. Then decide. And if you decide to leave, exit with grace. It is a cliché to say when people leave "our paths will cross again." It is utterly, totally true. Former colleagues and employers are a critical part of your career ecosystem. They will provide ratings and opinions about you for years to come. They will shop for talent in their current companies and in future places they work. They will become consultants, clients, and influencers. Wrap up your assignments with notable diligence and accountability. Heal wounds as appropriate. Say thank you.

2

TACTICS
THROUGH
THE STAGES

CHAPTER 8

Stage One—Starting Strong

"Not all those who wander are lost" —J.R.R. Tolkien

Some people know exactly what they want to do, and quickly land a satisfying job right out of school. They are "unicorns." Most of us are not unicorns. Very few people know exactly what they want to do, especially when just starting out. I started out in accounting, but soon fell in love with marketing and have spent the rest of my career pursuing that field. One of my daughters did a PhD in medieval history at Cambridge, and is now working as a researcher in the financial services industry in London.

As Adam Grant says in *Give and Take*: "I wish people had more realistic expectations early on in their careers." The whole first stage—often up to fifteen years—is a process of learning and discovery, of trial and error. It is not about finding some mythical job that you adore everyday. It is about finding out what you are good at, what you are bad at, what you love to do and what you hate. Stage One is not just about passively aging and "getting more seasoning" like some kind of steak. It is highly active and purposeful.

"A career is never a straight, upward-sloping line—often we need to go backward to go forwards, to get worse to get better, to invest to progress; the best journeys are those where we get lost" (Mark Moody-Stuart). The strategy for Stage One is simple: get in the game, embrace discovery, and build some fuel for the long journey ahead. That's it. If you can leave Stage One with that accomplished, you are in great shape. But executing the strategy is no easy task, so here are some practical ideas on how to do it.

Get in The Game

The first step in a career is to get in the game. Yet so many people find it hard to even find the starting line of Stage One.

Tara, a Masters student who will soon be graduating in London, lists some of the worries that she and her fellow students face:

- "What do I do if I'm not sure what I want to do for the rest of my life?"
- "This industry is so confusing. What sector of it might be most appealing?"
- "Am I qualified enough? Will I be good enough to succeed in the role if I don't have much practical experience?"
- "Will I fit into the company culture? Will they sponsor me for a visa (international students)?"

- "Will it help me achieve my long-term career goals?"
- "Will it pay the bills and help me pay back student loans?"
- "How do I know if I'll even like it?"

Parents are always willing to offer career help, but it has become increasingly difficult to pass on job-searching wisdom from a previous generation. A career conversation fifteen years ago between parent and child may have sounded something like this: "Hey Dad, I got an on-campus interview with AT&T in sales. What do you think—and doesn't Aunt Jennifer work there?" Today, it is more likely to sound like: "Dad, I just connected with the CEO of Strawberry Warthog Digital on LinkedIn. I'm thinking of going into their performance marketing division. But I can't figure out if I should focus on social or analytics." Most parents wouldn't understand a single word of that second conversation. It is no wonder that so many aspiring career-minded professionals (and their parents) are struggling.

For first-time job seekers like Tara, you need the right mind-set. It is a *war*. You are competing for scarce positions. The competition (increasingly global) is at least as smart and charming and talented as you are. Nobody owes you a job. Expect rejection, and lots of it.

Here are a few tips for people approaching the job market for the first time.

1. Use your school years to build early forms of fuel. I do not believe that school years should be a programmed way to get some predetermined job, but they certainly can lay the foundation for successful career options down the road.

The key point is not which exact courses you take, or your GPA to the third decimal place, or which organizations you get accepted into. What matters is the foundation you build for the future. Higher learning is a huge investment. Take advantage of this wonderful opportunity to accumulate:

> **Transportable skills**—As a body of learning, does your course selection give you critical skills that you can use in the future—problem solving, team work, curiosity, and more?

> **Meaningful experiences**—Are you using your college years to explore extra-curricular, leadership, travel, and internship opportunities that will equip you for the future?

> **Enduring relationships**—Are you meeting people and creating relationships with classmates, teachers, experts, mentors, and others you would like to stay connected to ten and twenty years into the future?

2. Create your job search battle plan. Build a spreadsheet and a database to help you land that first job. The battle plan will help you stay focused and active. Start by creating an initial list of perhaps ten to twenty companies that you think *might* be of interest to you based on the industry, location, size, company reputation, and recommendations from friends, family, career guidance counselors, etc. Then start building individual connections with this target list of companies and industries. With all of your target firms, document the contact information, including the company website, e-mail addresses, LinkedIn profiles, and phone numbers as you secure them. Keep track of the actions you take with each company, and any responses or next steps. Always highlight the application deadlines.

As your job search progresses, new avenues will open up and some companies and contacts will be added to your active target list. Some doors will also close, and those can be moved to the background exhibits. This is a healthy and necessary process. Keep a manageable list of active opportunities. Don't be overwhelmed by trying to keep hundreds of leads active at the same time.

3. Enthusiastically participate in on-campus recruiting. Many colleges and universities have on-campus recruiting sessions. I urge people to attend as many as possible. They offer up a flavor for the industry and the company that is hard to get just from a brochure or website. Sometimes, it is just good to see the kind of companies and industries you do *not* want to work for. And if you like the firm, try to make a one-to-one connection—get a business card, note an e-mail address, or think of a follow-up question. Use the on-campus recruiting resource center. You cannot depend on them to get you a job (that's up to you) but they are a great place to build basic skills and to rehearse for the big ugly world out there.

4. Become highly efficient at online applications. Web searches plus your own research will let you know who is hiring for specific jobs. Naturally, apply. Note the deadlines. Almost all have online applications before any interviews. Show your draft application to one or more of your trusted advisors—someone who works in the company or at least in the industry. Refine it and take your best shot. Online applications are frustrating because they are so anonymous and have very low response rates. You may need to do dozens or hundreds to land your first full-time job. Get over it. Online applications are an inevitable and necessary part of your job search battle plan. For some jobs they are the only way to get in the game. Just become very efficient at them. Do a smart, competent job and move on.

Rather than spending four hours "perfecting" that cover letter that no one may ever read, why not reinvest the time to find fifteen new personal connections for your job hunt.

5. Most importantly, leverage your connections. It is true in marketing, and certainly in job hunting, that having a relationship dramatically increases your response rates. Leverage your connections (mentors, alumni connections, friends, parents, other family members, neighbors). Use them to help you understand the options. Use them to sharpen your own sense of "fit" with certain industries, roles, and companies. Use them to open doors.

Create a long list of connections you believe could help you. Rank them—friends and acquaintances who have recently been hired into the industry are excellent. People who are senior leaders currently employed in the field are always good. And don't forget people who know you well and are your champions. They will be encouraging and really try to help you succeed. And they will have a better sense of "fit" than people who are in the industry but don't know you well.

One excellent way to build more contacts is to leverage both your alumni network and talent databases like LinkedIn.

Search your alumni directory to find out which members of your alumni association work in your target companies. And search LinkedIn to find people who work in a target company and went to the same school as you. If you can find a connection, reach out to them. You would be amazed at how many people are willing to talk about their jobs. Now, start working down your list. A great first step is a brief, personalized e-mail:

> Dear X,
>
> I am _____. I am writing to you at the suggestion of (mutual connection).
>
> I have begun my job search and am extremely interested in learning more about industry X. I would really value your advice. Would it be possible to arrange a twenty-minute call or meeting in the next week?
>
> I would be extremely grateful for any advice you can offer.
>
> Regards,
> Your contact info
> Your CV attached

That's it. Maybe include a sentence on one special thing you've done that might be of interest to this person. Do not overdo it. Don't ramble on about industry issues that you know little about. Don't regale the reader with long-winded anecdotes or platitudes. Get to the point. Be respectful. Suggest an easy next step.

You should ask for a small commitment of their time (fifteen to thirty minutes), because most of your connections will be wildly busy. You should suggest a time soon (in the next week or so) because it suggests respectful urgency. They'll either say yes or ignore it. If they say yes, you can work out whether it's a call or a meeting and whether it is ten minutes or several hours. My advice is to take what is offered, and use it to maximum advantage. If you don't hear back within four or five days, do not panic. Send a very brief follow-up, attaching your original note and the CV.

> Dear X,
>
> I am still extremely interested in getting your advice on the Y industry.
>
> Would it be possible to do a twenty-minute call this week or next? I would sincerely appreciate any perspective and advice you can offer.
>
> Regards,
>
> Your contact info
>
> Your CV attached

Not everyone will respond. This is perfectly fine. Welcome to the world of rejection. But a few will. Then what?

6. Before you meet your connections, do some homework. In the world of Wikipedia and LinkedIn it is inexcusable to not know at least the basics about the person you are talking to and the industry they work in. Every encounter is an interview, even if you think it is a casual chat. Prepare questions. Take notes. Write thank-you e-mails. Your connections are wondering whether to stick their necks out for you. Make it an easy decision for them. Spend as much time preparing intelligent questions as you spend preparing answers.

Some good questions people have asked me:

- What's different about this industry?
- What do you like/dislike about your job?
- What kinds of skills are required to succeed in your business?
- How did you get your job?
- What is the culture of your company, and how is it different from others?
- How do people today get into your industry? (Could be different from the past)
- What challenges keep you awake at night?
- Who do you consider the leaders in the industry?
- Do you know of any suitable open jobs in your company? (It's okay to ask.)

And the magic question you must always *always* ask:

- Is there someone else (a company, person) you would recommend that I talk to?

7. But finding a first job is so hard! If someone tells you about how hard a time they are having finding a job, you should send them to Bill Forrester[7] and Linda Turner of Goodwill Industries. In their respective roles as CEO and EVP of Goodwill Industries of New York, between them Bill and Linda have worked a total of sixty years in the job training business, and their teams have placed over 100,000 candidates. The jobseekers that Bill and Linda work with face extremely tough barriers. How would you like to try to land a

---

7 Bill has since retired after a distinguished 35+ year career with Goodwill Industries. In Spring 2016, the organization named Katy Gaul-Stigge as its new CEO.

job when you face a barrier like a developmental disability, or mental health issues, or can't afford transportation to get to the workplace, or language barriers? More poignantly, what if you tried to win a job interview on an empty stomach, or with a criminal record, or without decent clothes and haircut? The team at Goodwill has found success with what they call a "strengths-based model." They always start by focusing on the individual's strengths, capabilities, and skills. This builds the most essential starting point: a sense of confidence. To Bill and Linda, this is the central premise for success. With preparation, coaching, and the acknowledgment of small victories, it can be built up. Then, they work with the person to clearly identify the barriers to employment and systematically knock them down. What constructive steps can they take to overcome basic barriers like the lack of childcare, public transportation, language skills, computer literacy, and appearance? One of Goodwill's clients was a young man with autism. In most job situations, he would struggle very hard to succeed. But Goodwill discovered that he was skilled at and happy classifying colors. He found a job sorting and restocking merchandise at a retail clothing chain.

We all can learn a lot from Bill, Linda, and the team at Goodwill. Linda says: "Behind every job-search success are two things: the will to succeed, and a supportive group of connectors and champions." To increase the chances of success, Goodwill points their jobseekers to the most fertile hunting grounds. They study the market for high-demand job areas (Labor Market Report, ZipRecruiter) and point candidates towards these paths. It's not always the obvious or most prestigious jobs that have the highest demand. Linda believes that for her candidates there are many great nonacademic pathways to pursue—like electrician, plumber, and home health aide. What are the hot-demand job areas in your chosen field?

Finally, Goodwill finds that small successes (like getting a first interview or receiving a certificate for a new skill) really make a difference in building momentum and confidence. No one ever got a job on the first try. Most e-mails go ignored. Interviews get cancelled. Job openings get delayed, or vanish completely.

Here's the big message I take away from the brave job-hunters at Goodwill. It is tough out there. But none of us can whine about how tough we have it. Someone else always has it tougher. Go into battle, stick with your plan, and you will get in the game.

8. Discovery. Even once you land your first job, the process of discovery isn't over. It has just begun. You need to find out what you're good at, what you like to do, and what the world appreciates.

In his TEDx talk, author Robert Greene counsels us to be patient and open during the early years of our careers. The early years should be devoted to building competencies, experiences, and relationships. Greene observes that it invariably takes ten trials and nine errors to reach one success. It takes experimentation to identify a true passion, path, or purpose. He urges people early in their careers to tune in to what opportunities are presenting themselves to you, and also how you react—what you pay attention to, where you put your energy, which voices you listen to, and what you choose to read.[8]

As we think about people in Stage One of their careers, many of us admire the successful young entrepreneur. They appear to have discovered their passion and their big idea right out of the starting gates. Some observers wonder if they were just lucky.

It's a little more complicated than that. I have yet to meet an entrepreneur who actually succeeded with their first idea. And every single one of them have fought doubters and made big sacrifices.

Meet Alex White.

Profile: The Sweet Sound of Success

ALEX WHITE
Age 29

Role	CEO and cofounder of Next Big Sound (now part of Pandora Music)
Sweet Spot	The intersection of mathematics, data, and music

Alex White, the twenty-nine-year-old CEO of Next Big Sound, looks upbeat. He has good reason to be. His start-up, which analyzes consumer data for the music industry, was recently acquired by Pandora for an estimated $50 million. For Alex, it's an incredible payoff for twelve years of hard

---

8   See Robert Greene's TEDx talk, "The Key to Transforming Yourself," www.tedxtalks.ted.com/video/The-key-to-transforming-yoursel.

work and persistence in a notoriously difficult industry: the business of music.

"I initially wanted to be a rock star," he says with a grin. As the son of a professional cellist, he remembers growing up surrounded by music. In his teens, he juggled two part-time jobs at a bagel shop and a recording studio, where he would use the studio to record his own music between midnight and 5:00 a.m. "I realized that I didn't like performing my own songs around people. So if I couldn't be the rock star, I wanted to *find* the rock star, and that's when I switched my focus from the artist side to the business side. My dream was to work at a record label."

As a young student, Alex excelled at math and music composition. He attended Northwestern University because of its world-class music and business programs and soon set his sights on interning at a major music label. "I had a friend who was interning at Universal Music. I basically hounded him endlessly until he introduced me to the right people. I got an internship at Universal's New York offices, working in the Motown division."

He continued to hone his skills in radio production, events, and booking talent. He had a hip-hop radio show that aired from midnight to 2:30 a.m. every week, and headed the university's music programming board, where he booked concerts with major artists on campus. As an intern at Universal Records, he focused his sights on learning what he could from the company's top executives. "I kept begging them for five minutes, asking them 'How did you get here?'"

He expected to hear stories of slaving away in mailrooms and paying your dues over years, but what he learned surprised him. "Many of them had started their own labels that were then bought by Universal," he said. "That was the first time it occurred to me that I needed to start something. I was always making and selling things, but I had never heard the word entrepreneurship before."

He started reading everything he could about the industry, but the economic climate in 2005 made it impossible to start a label. That's when inspiration struck. "If I want to sign bands, and all the interns I work with also want to be record moguls, maybe we could create a site where anyone could create a record label, and we could use social media to track how early you could identify real talent." This is what would become the first iteration of Next Big Sound—a type of fantasy sports site for music, where users could use their instincts to predict what breakthrough artist was going to emerge on the scene next. "I thought it was the best idea, and I was paranoid that someone was going to take it and build it first." He found two technical cofounders and the three of them spent the next three years developing the concept.

Alex, by then in his senior year of college, had received a job offer from a consulting firm in New York that was scheduled to start in the fall. He made a deal with his cofounders: if they could raise $30,000, they would quit their jobs and work on the new business full-time. "I pushed my job's start date back as much as I could, and spent my $10,000 signing bonus on Next Big Sound."

Through the help of his network, including his entrepreneurship professor, Alex was able to raise $25,000, which, the team agreed, was close enough to make the leap. He used some of that capital to repay the consulting firm's signing bonus, and rejected their offer. "They thought I was crazy to say no," he recalls. The week afterwards, just as

Alex and the team were ramping up to start raising $150,000 in funds, the economy had its now-infamous meltdown of 2008.

When asked to describe what went through his mind when he turned down a stable job for a risky venture in unforgiving market conditions, he shrugs. "I kept thinking that if I took the job and someone else launched this idea, I would have literally killed myself. I couldn't live with the idea of having missed this opportunity. I would wake up every morning in a panic and google it, to see if someone else had invented it. A consulting gig would always be there." He looks thoughtful. "It wasn't the glory, but an urgency to do it first."

The next few years were filled with setbacks. In 2008 the team applied to TechStars, a Colorado based start-up incubator, but was rejected. Their site had thousands of bands and users, but site visits were flattening out, and the team was running out of what little money they had. "We were crushed," Alex said. "I was just barely scraping by. I had budgeted twenty dollars per week for groceries, and forty dollars on the weekends for beer." Things got even more complicated when they reapplied to TechStars the following year and were accepted—only to realize they no longer wanted to pursue the original concept for Next Big Sound. Luckily, TechStars understood, and the team took the next few weeks to figure out their next step.

"We tried a few ideas within the first month, and started to collect some data points. We realized the music industry was not looking at online numbers, just tracking CD sales. We launched a basic version of Next Big Sound where we used screen-scraping robots to figure out what could be useful to music industry professionals." The social media metrics space was being overlooked, and Alex realized it could provide valuable insights to managers, labels, and talent. The idea took off, and everything started moving fast. They raised $1 million, grew the team to six and then nine people. Alex and his cofounders were finally able to pay themselves a $50,000 salary. A Series A round of $6.5 million allowed Next Big Sound to double in size and they started working with bands directly.

In July of 2015, Next Big Sound was acquired by Pandora. Modest and down to earth, Alex is quick to point out the role that luck played in his success as well. "The number of things that went our way was terrifying," he said shaking his head. "If you want to start your own company just so you can be on the Forbes Under 30 list, it's not worth it. If you want to be an entrepreneur to make a lot of money, don't. If you find something you're obsessed with, something that keeps you up at night, then that's the thing you should pursue."

Not many of us may be math and music geniuses like Alex, but there is a lot we can draw from his story. What really struck me about Alex's journey was the combination of unshakeable passion and constant openness. He kept his eyes on the prize, but relentlessly adapted his approach. There was no question that Alex was obsessed with getting his idea to succeed, and he made some real sacrifices. He turned down a really solid job and gave back the sign-on bonus during a recession. He couch-surfed with friends and lived on a few dollars a day. Yet he was open to advice and improvements to his idea every day. He credits mentors like his entrepreneurship professor Troy Henikoff and his TechStars advisor Jason Mendelson with tirelessly challenging his thinking and pushing him to make it better. They helped him with cosmic business model questions but also practical tactics—like how to draft a sensitive e-mail to an investor or partner. Alex depended upon his cofounders David Hoffman and Samir Rayani for intellectual input but also emotional support: "They were right there going through it with me as cofounders. They were the only ones who could really understand the challenges and stress of what we were trying to do." During our interview, Alex passed along a great quote: "Days should be rigorously planned, and the nights left open to chance". It reminds us all to make sure we keep some serendipity in our lives. Alex credits luck as a big factor in his success. But he didn't find success at the intersection of music and math just by chance. Luck favors the well-prepared mind.

Stage One: Starting Strong—Summary

Whether you pursue a predominantly entrepreneurial or corporate pathway, use Stage One to establish good career habits and take on fuel. The most important thing is to become "the brand manager of you." Whether you like it or not, employers constantly shop for talent. And how you treat your career will determine whether you are on the menu when they go shopping. We can learn a lot from how brands are built. It is not a trick or shortcut. Leading brands are built on quality ingredients and crafted with care. Being flashy and promotional can be a good way to win initial trials of your product, but enduring brands consistently deliver what is promised on the package. When leading brands fail to perform, they fix it.

As your own personal brand manager, use Stage One to create the building blocks and habits for a successful career. Get informed, get engaged, become an expert in something, learn to communicate effectively, build eminence, seek feedback, and build value.

For many employees, the only orientation they get is a few hours with the HR department going over the travel and entertainment policy and maybe a bit of company history. If you are serious about your career, this is not enough. Learn what makes your company tick: where it came from, what it stands for, how it makes its money, who the key people are, and where it is going. If you don't get answers to these questions as part of your company's normal indoctrination, make it your business to find out in the first hundred days. Do your homework. Read the company's annual report, or better yet, an outside analyst's assessment of the company. Ask both old-timers and rising stars to tell you the inside scoop on your company over a cup of coffee. Get engaged by joining a club, team, or professional network in the firm. Volunteer to help with a company event, and do it well. Slowly begin to build your career ecosystem of contacts, communities, critical colleagues, and champions.

Early in your career, choose a few topics to become an expert in, and become a "go-to" person. It doesn't need to be something earth shattering, just some question or topic that comes up frequently enough and where you have developed some special expertise. In my company, I know that if I ever have a question about sports marketing, I can go to Daniel. On millennial voting trends, I go to Izzy. On content management systems, I go to Ken. What's interesting is that the average age of Daniel, Izzy and Ken is not forty-eight, it is twenty-eight. They are deeply passionate and knowledgeable about their topics. And by volunteering for after-hours projects in our company, their special expertise is now visible to senior management.

A lot of young people ask how they can get more airtime with senior managers and clients. They feel they are being held back or sheltered from important exposure. The truth is that if they just went unprepared into a meeting with senior leaders, they would be crucified. If you are just sitting in a room taking notes, or asking naive questions, it does not help your cause—it harms it. It evokes responses like "Who was that person and why am I paying for them?" or "Who asked that question, we did it four years ago." Not exactly what you were going for.

Instead, why not work with your boss to find a very specific question that your senior leader or client is grappling with. Quietly take it on as a two-week assignment. Research the topic up, down, and sideways. Check your facts. Write your answer down into a crisp five-minute presentation. Bulletproof your argument and rehearse. Work with your boss to find the right time to get your five minutes of stage time with the heavyweights. Pitch your brains out. Listen intently for feedback. Repeat. By doing this every couple of months, you will become a trusted go-to person on a growing list of topics. This builds equity in your career.

Another early habit to build is effective communication. Regardless of what role and industry we are in, nothing defines people's perceptions of us like how we communicate. Take every opportunity early in your career to hone your skills—not just what you say, but how you say it and where you say it.

Most people are lousy communicators. You can stand out by becoming one of those rare individuals who communicate clearly, and can tell an interesting story. To improve clarity, I coach people to write down a quick outline before any communication—-even a minor one. First, what is the topic? Our audiences are changing gears from e-mail to e-mail and meeting to meeting so rapidly that half the time they literally don't even know what we are talking about. Make it crystal clear every time. Next, write down your three main points, with supporting facts and reasons to believe you. This means you have a point of view and some evidence to back it up. Finally, say exactly what you want the audience to do next. If you do this, at least your communications will be strong and clear. That will set you ahead of about 80 percent of the working world.

To make yourself really special, become a good storyteller. Not everyone has the gift, but with practice, we can all become competent storytellers. To me, the keys are the use of simple, evocative imagery and the ability to create human empathy. I love listening to podcasts and The Moth. I watch videos of masters of public speaking and persuasion like Bill Clinton and Steve Jobs. I critique my own speeches on video. Study, do, and learn.

One of my pet peeves in business is that even if people have the right messages, they often choose the wrong medium to convey them. E-mail is a magnificent way to rapidly disseminate factual, emotionally neutral information.

"The meeting is at noon in room 7B," or "The budget spreadsheet is attached." E-mail is a terrible way to defuse an emotionally charged issue. Think about it. In your entire life, have you ever actually *solved* a difficult emotional issue with an e-mail? If you are like me and millions of others, I'll bet that many times you have escalated the violence of an emotional issue via e-mail. The easiest way, of course, is with the dreaded "Reply All" button.

The point is simple: you cannot defuse an emotional issue with an emotionally-neutral medium. Emoticons help a bit, but e-mail and text are still lousy ways to resolve tough emotional conflict. That requires old-school channels like the telephone and face-to-face time. It's okay to use text or e-mail as the set-up medium, but use something more personal as the closer: "Wow. This is a really important issue. We must talk. Can we meet or talk by phone at 9:00 a.m. tomorrow?" A voice medium like the phone can work to resolve tough issues because it has at least some emotional component. Skype can sometimes be better than voice alone, but only if the transmission quality is good. Face-to-face meetings remain the most precious and expensive of all communication forms. I find that it is wasted on mundane meetings where there is little or no emotional content. But until we invent something better, it remains by far the best way resolve a truly emotional issue.

One final thought on the written word. Even as the world has gone digital, there is a beautiful role for the written word. In a sea of e-mails and text messages, think of the impact that a small piece of paper, written in your own hand, will have on your audience. I still send the occasional postcard, handwritten note, or letter because it is the best way to mark an emotional moment of truth. In business and in life, what a great way to convey feelings like "Congratulations," "We're glad you're here," "Thank you," "I am sorry," and "My condolences."

At some point in Stage One you can invest time and effort in building your social eminence—your reputation on the social platforms and in the industry at large. Do you have an active voice on the social platforms affecting your industry, and do others seem influenced by your views? Your social eminence can be built by joining industry associations, by blogging, and by speaking. These can be great ways to increase your expertise and career ecosystem. Just make sure you have built up your fundamentals first. You want to springboard off a strong product, some genuine expertise, and a solid reputation in your own firm.

You will need to take active steps in Stage One to ensure that your reputation is strong. Some employers are great at giving candid and constructive feedback. Most are not. Take accountability for seeking and responding to feedback. Find out the six to ten factors that really matter in performing your job. Ask for feedback on your performance as well as your style. Many companies and bosses struggle with giving candid feedback on "style" issues. A technique I have found useful to give employees concrete and constructive feedback on style is built around what Aristotle called the "golden mean." Aristotle believed that virtues live in the middle ground between two extremes, so that Bravery was the golden mean that lived between the extremes of Cowardice on one end and Recklessness on the other.

I've found this helpful in providing feedback on leadership style issues because it doesn't say to the employee,

"You are a bad leader," it says, "Here are the leadership dimensions we are talking about, here's where you stand today, and here is the direction you need to be moving." I call it a "napkin nudge" because I often write it down on a napkin or a sheet of paper and use it to nudge the individual to a more successful behavior. All I can say is, it works.

Below is an actual example of a "napkin nudge" I used to counsel a young leader on her personal style. We thought about some of the dimensions of her style that were really important to her success. I then put an X beside where I thought she was on each dimension and counseled her to move in a certain direction—towards the ideal. She then

LEADERSHIP STYLE GUIDANCE

TOO LITTLE	IDEAL	TOO MUCH

Pushover	→ Strong & Warm ←	Pushy
Plodding	→ Dynamic ←	Frantic
In The Weeds	→ Well-Engaged ←	In The Clouds
Fort Knox	→ Selective ←	Facebook

Plot where you currently stand, then set a personal goal to move closer to the Ideal

Pushover → Strong & Warm ← Pushy

could think about concrete ways to move her profile, and to periodically check in on her progress. She was perceived as a bit timid and a micromanager, though surprisingly, she tended to overshare personal details in the workplace in a way that others found concerning. This exercise helped her to elevate and round out her style.

I find that when I use very simple language and images like "pushy vs. pushover" and "in the weeds vs. in the clouds" that people grasp and accept the feedback more readily. The last one, "Fort Knox vs. Facebook", is about how readily people share information at work. I use Fort Knox to mean too little, and Facebook to mean too much.

The final skill in Stage One is to understand your value and how to be fairly rewarded for your contributions. Many people early in their careers are naive and ill-prepared for these conversations. They often get bad advice from coworkers, family members, or recruiters.

My advice is simple. First, getting the right compensation and recognition is about contribution, not the calendar. No one owes you a raise or a promotion because of the passage of time. It does not matter than Jennifer got a raise after sixteen months and you are passing the eighteen-month mark on Tuesday. It is about the value you are bringing to the company. Understand what is expected from you in your role and deliver it superbly. When you are looking to have your performance and compensation reviewed, start by writing up your contributions. Include both "hard" contributions and soft metrics. Did you generate revenue for the firm, bring in a new client, or help save the company money? Is there evidence that you made the company's customers happier? Did you invent a valuable new product, idea, or process that will someday increase profit? Perhaps you have done something that adds to the company's reputation (published an article, given a well-rated speaking event, won an award, etc.) or made some important additions to the talent pool. As much as possible, talk about outcomes, not just activities. Just doing your job only qualifies you to continue in your current role and pay.

Book one-on-one time with your boss and ideally also at least one of your mentors. Ask if you are focused on the right priorities and goals—the real stuff that is of value to the company and its business, not just marginal pet projects. Ask how well you are performing relative to your peers. Ask what more you could be doing, and what it will take to get to the next step.

If you are going to push for a raise or promotion, go in on a win. If you expect to get promoted, think about some candidates who could credibly replace you in your current job. If you are a good performer, your boss will have some natural resistance to moving you into a new role. Make it easy for them to support your move by proposing some options around your succession plan. If a promotion is not forthcoming, set a plan and a timetable with your boss that could change the outcome. If you still don't like the answer, do some career pathway thinking and look at your other options. As you are looking at options, stick to the big picture. In Stage One, ask yourself—what is going to give me the greatest learning curve and the maximum career equity—the net positive energy being created in your career.

In the chapter on career ecosystems, we talked about how mentorship can be one of the most powerful career accelerants. Keep this in mind during Stage One, because you cannot start too early. And one of the most powerful accelerants of mentorship is a cup of coffee. Meet Dave Wilkin.

Profile: Connecting with Mentors

DAVID WILKIN
Age 26

Role	Founder and CEO, TenThousandCoffees.com
Sweet Spot	Bringing together the world's millennials and business leaders

It's easy to underestimate the impact of something as simple as sharing a cup of coffee with someone. It's a near-universal ritual that is intergenerational and non-threatening. It facilitates an easy sharing of ideas and information in an informal setting. It's a meeting that offers tremendous potential.

For David Wilkin, a coffee date with Mia Pearson, an entrepreneur and mentor, gave him the push he needed to start his own business. "I grew up in a small town with no network for what I wanted to do, and so when I was finishing school I e-mailed a number of different industry leaders and asked them to go to coffee with them and talk about what opportunities are out there. I e-mailed Mia, who is also from Northern Ontario, and we were able to have such a great conversation," he said. "It turned into the best opportunity I ever could have imagined and it happened over a cup of coffee.

"Within five minutes of that cup of coffee [Mia] had me completely clear on my next steps—on what to do to change how the next generation could unlock opportunity," Dave said in a recent interview. He believes that coffee is a wonderful way to propel careers, and wants to help other young people unlock this same opportunity for themselves.

David is the founder and CEO of a global platform called Ten Thousand Coffees, a free social network that connects young people with skilled professionals and invites them to exchange ideas and advice over a cup of coffee. "It's a global social experiment where we connect millions of millennials with companies and educational institutions and create connections and conversations where insights can flow."

Ten Thousand Coffees now has active users in more than twenty-five major cities and connects them to a growing roster of mentor-leaders including CEOs, scientists, astronauts, TV personalities, bankers, and even the Prime Minister of Canada, Justin Trudeau. The platform also counts over a thousand companies who want to connect better with the next generation of talent and consumers. Unlike big job fairs, coffee dates provide one-on-one engagement resulting in a higher quality of connection and profound mentoring relationships. "That's what this is all about—making it easier for the leaders of today to meet the leaders of tomorrow," he said, and in order to do that, we have to tackle the current system of mentorship that exists today—a system that David believes is broken.

"Everyone knows that mentorship is important. But the current model isn't scalable or sustainable. It's limited to like-minded individuals within one's personal network," he explained in a recent blog post. "Ten Thousand Coffees is changing that. We're bringing the traditional model of mentorship into the twenty-first century. We like to think of it as a win-win because Ten Thousand Coffees is designed to unleash opportunities that may or may not have otherwise been possible." David's Ten Thousand Coffees platform is inherently a two-way street. The young advice seekers get what they are looking for, but so do the leader-experts. Blue-chip companies are using the platform to engage their employees internally. They find it's a really good way to get research input into their innovation and product development projects, and to connect senior managers and young employees within the firm. Alumni associations are using Ten Thousand Coffees to keep the institution connected to their alumni tribe and to make it easy for students and alumni to connect around mutual interests.

David has managed to capture the tangible value of a face-to-face meeting through the use of digital tools. Thanks to the platform, it is now easy for people who wouldn't normally meet to get together. The young mentees search the platform for an expert leader who can provide relevant advice. Then they write up a request outlining their background and the advice they are seeking. The platform then makes it really convenient for both parties to connect and schedule a meeting or call together. It wasn't the first time David had turned to technology to connect communities: in high school, the self-described math and science geek created a networking platform to connect the school to alumni.

Despite already being a founder and CEO well before his thirtieth birthday, David, who's from a small town in rural Canada, had humbler aspirations growing up: to be the first person in his family to attend college. He dreamed of pursuing his ambitions in the big city and knew that an education could be his ticket to a brighter future. He spent a summer writing scholarship applications, and was accepted into the University of Waterloo on a full scholarship, majoring in Biochemistry.

During his first summer as a college student, the only job the university could help him secure was as a minimum-wage dishwasher. Thinking he could rustle up more interesting opportunities himself, David applied for and was hired as a government spokesperson for youth. In this role, David did research into the needs of Canadian youth and acted as their voice to policymakers. He started building relationships with companies and learning about public speaking, PR, and communications. From the beginning, David was building skills and relationships that would prove useful later on.

It was during his third year of college that he had that fateful coffee date with his mentor, Mia Pearson. "At that moment, when she saw that opportunity, she stopped me and said 'You need to go start a company.' She actually said, 'I'm not going to talk to you again until you go and start a company. Go and do it.'"

Soon afterwards, David left school to pursue his own company full time, much to the shock and bewilderment of his family and friends. "They wanted to know if I'd lost my mind," David recalled, but he was ready to take the leap. "Life is not linear. It's not what you learn in the classroom. It's what you learn outside. And the best work happens when you're not working." David's first company was a marketing agency devoted to helping companies and governments improve their marketing to millennials. After two years, David knew that he could make a decent living by working hard at his agency, but he wanted to build something really ambitious and lasting. That was when he knew he wanted to build a business around the Ten Thousand Coffees idea.

For David, focusing on helping young people has always been a strong narrative in his own career path, a pursuit he finds incredibly rewarding. "Youth is the future. For companies, over 50 percent of their workforce will be millennials in the next five years or so. Brands are spending millions of dollars on digital and social marketing, which was completely disrupted and created by millennials. Governments around the world are facing elections where youth will cast the deciding vote," he explained. "When you look at all those things you realize how important it is for young people to have a better way to share their ideas and gain insights and take their first step."

David's ambition now is to take Ten Thousand Coffees to every school, company, and region to help the next generation get access to the people they need to be successful. He believes that success should be measured by the size of the problems people try to solve. "There are so many big problems that need solutions," he said. "Take advantage of opportunities. Find a problem so important to you that you will cry if it doesn't get solved."

The David Wilkin story offers several important lessons for Stage One. David was not born with connections or a career ecosystem, so he created one for himself. He invented opportunities for himself so that he could get in the game. He built transportable skills and became a go-to expert on an important topic. He found a mentor, took some risks, and started to turn his dream into reality. He did not get the idea right the first time around, but was able to discover, adapt, and persevere. These are the hallmarks of a great career start in Stage One.

CHAPTER 9

Stage Two—Reaching High

"Build on the islands of strength." —Peter Drucker

"To thine own self be true." —Polonius,
in Shakespeare's *Hamlet*

Stage Two—which begins approximately fifteen years into a career—brings with it some unique opportunities and anxieties. How high can I go, and how do I navigate the next step? How do I find my sweet spot, but avoid getting bored and stale? How do I increase my impact without just working longer hours and wrecking my life? How do I convert all of that great groundwork in Stage One into some meaningful rewards? Stage Two is the time to identify, feed, and bet on your strengths. It's when you must learn to operate at scale so that your impact is magnified. The most successful leaders in Stage Two do an excellent job aligning their passions and core strengths—and largely ignoring their weaknesses.

If Stage One is about discovering your sweet spot, then Stage Two is about nailing it. Keep asking those three hard questions: What am I good at? What do I love to do? What does the world appreciate?

In Stage One we talked about building expertise, accumulating transportable skills, and becoming a go-to resource for certain topics. Stage Two is about creating true differentiation. Dorie Clark, author and professor at Duke University, urges us to "stand out." The consulting firm McKinsey looks for "spiking" in a talent profile—areas of skill and passion that are way above average. Once we understand what makes us different, we need to spend time on it, nurture it, and celebrate it.

One of my favorite career moments came when my employee Kathy Ryan came into my office one day and said that she had appointed herself CEO and had the business cards to prove it. This was a bit cheeky, because Kathy was an executive in our firm, but I was definitely the Chief Executive Officer. Kathy explained that I shouldn't be worried, because on her business card, CEO meant Chief Execution Officer. Kathy had decided after long experience and reflection that the thing she was absolutely fantastic at was execution. Others may choose more glamorous pathways, but Kathy knew her special gift was getting things done. She declared her specialty with pride, and it was tremendously helpful in her career. People always knew who to turn to for execution, and Kathy was always at the top of the list. Kathy is now officially retired, but remains one of the most in-demand consultants I have ever met. Whenever she gets tired of playing golf in Florida, she has a long list of suitors who want to hire this master executor for well-paid assignments from Texas to Paris to Cape Town.

Robert Greene has written eloquently on the subject of mastery and its role in the central stage of our careers. "In our twenties and maybe even in our thirties, we can do pretty well in our work, even though it is not a passionate interest. We are young and have energy; we get satisfaction mostly from outside work. But eventually our lack of deep connection to the field catches up with us, often in our forties. We feel increasingly disengaged and not challenged. Our natural creative energies have gone fallow. We fail to pay attention to the changes going on in our field because we are disconnected. People younger, more creative, and less expensive quickly replace us."

Greene adds that the secret ingredients to creating mastery are desire and time. "We all know how much more deeply we learn when we are motivated. If a subject excites us, if it stirs our deepest curiosity, or if we have to learn because the stakes are high, we pay much more attention. What we absorb sinks in. If we find ourselves in France needing to learn the language, or suddenly in love with a French woman who speaks little English, we can learn more in a few months than four years of French classes, no matter how good the teacher. In other words, our level of focus will determine the depth of our learning."

Greene believes that mastery is not genetic. If we multiply deep concentration over enough time, we can master anything. He believes that mastery seems to require 10,000 hours—or even 20,000 hours if we are seeking grand mastery. "To apply yourself to a field or to a problem for that long a time means there will inevitably be moments of boredom and tedium. Practice, particularly in the beginning, is never exciting. To persist past these moments you have to feel love for the field. You have to feel passionately excited by the prospect of discovering or inventing something new. Otherwise, you will give up. There is no mastery or power without passion. Through all of my research, that much I am certain about."

Greene goes on to cite historical examples of this—Darwin and the development of his theory of natural selection, Einstein and his theory of special relativity, Thomas Edison and the development of the electric light bulb, Henry Ford and the Model T, John Coltrane and the revolutionary music he came to produce, Martha Graham and the creation of modern dance, etc. A great contemporary example would be Steve Jobs. He was obsessed with technology and design since childhood. He went through a lengthy apprenticeship with his first period at Apple and then with NeXT, experiencing many failures and invaluable lessons. By the time he returned to Apple in 1996, he had come to master something almost intangible—the ability to sense trends well before others. This formula of desire multiplied by time can be applied to artists, athletes, chess players, inventors, biologists, and any other field.[9]

Todd Herman would certainly qualify as a master—of salesmanship. He didn't start out that way, but that is what he grew into. His story illustrates many of the principles of

---

9   See Robert Greene, "How to Become the Master of Any Skill," *Forbes*, November 13, 2012, www.forbes.com/sites/danschawbel/2012/11/13/robert-greene-how-to-become-the-master-of-any-skill/.

mastery and differentiation that are critical to Stage Two. Meet Todd:

Profile: Don't Sell Yourself Short

TODD HERMAN
Age 39

Role	CEO, The Peak Athlete, and "World's Greatest Salesperson"
Sweet Spot	The intersection of athletic coaching and business performance

There are some moments of your career that always stand out in your mind. For Todd Herman, being congratulated by Facebook founder Mark Zuckerberg on winning the World's Greatest Salesperson contest held at the 2010 Cannes Advertising Festival is one of those instances. In early 2010 my company conducted a global search for The World's Greatest Salesperson—to better understand and celebrate the art of selling in the twenty-first century. We issued an open challenge to salespeople everywhere: make the world's most persuasive two-minute YouTube video selling the benefits of an ordinary red brick. From thousands of entries, the top YouTube videos along with accompanying written essays on modern selling were evaluated by an expert panel of ten sales and marketing leaders. Todd was one of three finalists selected to fly to the south of France to pitch a new technology product to a live audience at the Cannes Advertising Festival. His pitch won the most votes, and he was awarded the title of World's Greatest Salesperson.

For Todd, a Canadian farm boy who spent his childhood feeding chickens and riding horses on his parents' cattle ranch in rural Alberta, this surreal victory was a culmination of years spent honing and refining his sales skills on what many would consider an unconventional career path. Today, Todd has developed his power to sell into a power that inspires others—he is a globally recognized performance coach, supporting athletes and businesses in their quests to become stronger, faster, and better.

Growing up, Todd had always possessed an amicable personality that served him well in his first job as a restaurant manager. One day, a customer suggested that he try his hand at sales, and Todd was intrigued. "My father always said if you're going to do something, find out who's the best and do it with them. At that time, the leaders in sales were IBM or Xerox." Todd applied to both companies but was turned down. He was disappointed, but undeterred. "I created a three-month proposal and convinced Xerox to let me work in their struggling printer division on a salary based 100 percent on commissions. I was super confident that I would ace it."

He didn't. In fact, he failed miserably, discovering that the talkative friendliness he had cultivated in customer service as a restaurant manager did not translate to sales. It got so bad that Todd's boss at Xerox called him the "greatest disappointment of my career." It was one of Todd's lowest moments professionally. "I learned an extremely valuable lesson about the importance of listening more than talking," he said. "I had to just shut up and sell."

In his mid-twenties, Todd read a copy of *Coaching the Mental Game* by H. A. Dorfman, a book about the vital link between mental awareness and athletic performance. Todd spotted an opportunity to apply his selling ability to motivating others and started a coaching company called The Peak Athlete, focusing on coaching young athletes to become stronger mentally, emotionally, and physically. He discovered that this style of coaching wasn't just valuable for athletes, but for businesses as well. "The parents of some of my athlete clients started asking me to come in and coach some of their talent, especially their customer services and sales teams."

Todd continued to hone his own selling and coaching skills by learning from the best in the business. He approached Jim Rohn, a respected writer and motivational speaker after one of his speeches. Todd asked Jim if he could work with him, even if it meant doing so for free. He applied the same approach to working with Harvey Dorfman, renowned sports coach and mentor to major athletes. "I offered to work for Harvey for free," he recalled. "I worked for him for a month in North Carolina, watching him in action and learning how he negotiated and worked with clients."

Todd's career has continued to thrive. Today, in addition to his athletic coaching business, he coaches and invests in entrepreneurial companies who are seeking higher performance. He studies his craft constantly. He writes and speaks at industry events to keep connected and sharp. He believes in skill sprints—periodically using cycles of ninety days to intensely focus on improving one specific ability. This is reflective of Todd's philosophy on success: it's a continuous process of constant improvement, or in his own words, having "big dreams and taking small steps forward." As long as you maintain a focused forward momentum, you'll continue to succeed, even in the face of setbacks. "Some things will fail," he said. "You can't really sugarcoat it. But you can decide whether or not to learn from it."

Todd turned a job in a restaurant and a series of rejections into a successful long-term career. I am always impressed by how hard Todd studies his craft. He constantly tests new hypotheses. I know for a fact that he fully wrote and produced three YouTube videos for the World's Greatest Salesperson contest, pre-tested the three among an expert panel of sales practitioners, and submitted the winner. We can all take a lesson from how he sought out the best, and made it incredibly easy—even free—for the best to teach him everything they know. Now, Todd has expanded his sweet spot from coaching athletic performance to coaching business performance.

If Todd Herman took a relatively circuitous route to get from where he started to where he ended up, think about the journey of Rachel Moore, who danced her way into the boardroom.

Profile: From Baryshnikov to Boardroom

RACHEL S. MOORE
Age 50

Role	Former CEO of the American Ballet Theatre, and now president & CEO of The Music Center, Los Angeles
Sweet Spot	The arts meets business

Rachel was born in Davis, California to parents who were both economists. An aspiring professional ballet dancer in her teens, Rachel's first career crossroads arose at age eighteen. The prestigious American Ballet Theatre (ABT) in New York City invited her to dance under the direction of Mikhail Baryshnikov. Should she go on to college in California, or become a professional dancer in far-away New York? Some of the people back home worried. "New York is too scary. You are doomed."

Rachel chose dance, Baryshnikov, and the ABT.

Rachel's early career as a ballerina flourished until age twenty-four, when she severely injured her ankle. Faced with the prospect of only being able to perform at 95 percent capacity and in constant pain, Rachel knew she needed to leave the ballerina life for something new. But what? Since she was twenty-four, most traditional top colleges would not accept her. Brown University was more open than most and offered her a scholarship in Philosophy. Not everybody back home thought it was a great idea. When Rachel graduated, she knew she still wanted to do something to help the arts— maybe become a lawyer. But a lawyer friend gave her some good advice: "If you really want to have impact on artists and the arts, help them with the business side. Work with arts organizations so they're running as good businesses and allowing artists to do their work."

So Rachel applied to business schools and earned her Masters in arts administration from Columbia University. For the next decade, Rachel built her early career as an arts administrator in Washington, DC and New England. To pay her dues, she helped mayors integrate the arts into their communities, ran a small ballet company, taught at a classical

music school for children of color and worked at the Boston
Ballet. Along the way, Rachel learned some tough lessons,
like the time she needed to tell her vendors that the payments
wouldn't just be a little late—the organization had absolutely
no money. "Experiences like that teach you who you are."
One of her saddest career lessons came during a nasty HR
dispute between a board member and staff. "The board
didn't do the right thing. I lost faith, and had to move on."

Rachel's career came full circle when American Ballet
Theatre, where she had debuted as a professional ballerina
almost twenty years earlier, approached her as a candidate
to become their executive director. The ABT job was big,
prestigious, and demanding. The budget was $45 million,
the staff numbered seven hundred, and the organization
was facing some serious challenges. Rachel was a dark horse
candidate. She was the youngest candidate, and the ABT had
never hired a woman or a former dancer into the top job.
She won the role and spent the next eleven and a half years
stabilizing and building the ABT. To round out her skills, she
took a fellowship program in non-profit leadership from the
Stanford University Graduate School of Business. "I think
what helped me at ABT was that I was tough and business
savvy enough to do union negotiations, but soft-handed
enough to appreciate the artists and the artistic agenda."
One of her proudest moments was championing Misty
Copeland, the first African American woman to be named
principal dancer in the ABT's seventy-five-year history.

Rachel's journey continues. In the past year, she has
written a book called *The Artist's Compass* (Touchstone, 2016)
and has taken on a big new role as president and CEO of
the Music Center in Los Angeles. Rachel's special mastery

lies at the intersection between the world of business and the world of the arts. She regularly mentors young artists, often teaching them basic survival skills. "In the past, a top graduate from a top institution like Juilliard would get a good union job in an orchestra and be pretty much set. The old world was a power structure that offered security and a clear path. If you were in, you were *in*." Today, even top grads from Juilliard struggle, but there are so many more pathways. Artists who are not entrepreneurial can find it painful. Rachel hates it when artists fail not because their work is bad, but because they are bad at self-marketing. Rachel always asks aspiring artists: "Why does what you are doing make a difference, and why should the world care?" She encourages young artists to challenge their assumptions on what it takes to have a sustainable career in the arts. "What is the value proposition of a $200,000-$300,000 degree at a top five arts school? If you are one of the truly lucky few who become a star, you make your ROI." But Rachel feels there is a much higher probability bet. "Find a program or a specific teacher who is great at what you want to do. This could easily be outside the famous tier one colleges. It is the teacher and the program that make it really worth it."

Rachel believes that "actor/waiter" is not the best career path. She feels that it really means "failed or distracted actor" versus a career with some acting in it. She encourages young artists to find related businesses that can keep them in and around their art. She is a big fan of jobs like teacher or accompanist where artists can make decent steady pay but still stay close to their passions. Increasingly, Rachel urges artists to develop their marketing skills and create their own e-commerce business. Managing your expenses is also a critical skill for the aspiring artist. Do you really need to live in New York, London, or Los Angeles to pursue your craft? Visual artists are thriving in Detroit, where average house prices are under $20,000.

For those who are aspiring not just to be artists but also to be top leaders in Arts administration, Rachel offers the following advice: "Know your financials. This is the Achilles' heel for most arts organizations. Understand a profit and loss statement, budgeting, and cost control. Also, know how to generate revenue, not just count it. Your first big job is to earn or raise money for the organization. Networking isn't crass. It is essential. It doesn't have to be about annoying people and begging. Make it about reciprocity and exchange." Rachel continues: "Have multiple mentors, and look outside the tiny sphere of your current organization and sector to the greater world. What can we learn from other domains? Don't burn bridges. Be nice. Be kind. I came back to a great job at the American Ballet Theatre after almost fifteen years. Finally, don't tell artists they are going to fail before they try. They are big boys and girls. The market will tell them."

I am always intrigued by people who find their sweet spots in the middle of their careers. On a frigid weekend night last January, I took a walking tour of Harlem along with my wife and one of my daughters. Along the way, the three of us and about a dozen other intrepid travelers from the US, the UK, and Australia visited the highlights of Harlem's storied jazz age. Over the course of the evening we dropped in to about six jazz bars, restaurants, and clubs and soaked up the history of Harlem's jazz scene past and present. Our host and tour guide for the evening was Gordon. Over a few cocktails, I learned Gordon's story. He'd started as a restaurateur, but after more than a few ups and downs and disappointing failures, Gordon landed on what he really wanted to do: share his love for the Harlem jazz scene with the world. He set up a company, Big Apple Jazz, and now hosts tours about two hundred days a year. His tours are among the top-rated things to do in New York. The Harlem music scene isn't just something Gordon is passionate about. He is good at it, and world is willing to pay money to share in his passion.[10]

Someone who started life in Harlem but has now moved on is Chuck Reese. Chuck built a career for himself from humble beginnings and in Stage Two is now facing the classic sole-proprietor's dilemma: how can he smooth out and scale up his business without just working longer or crazier hours? Meet Chuck Reese.

Profile: Doors Slammed, Doors Opened

CHUCK REESE
Age 45

Role	Graphic Designer, owner of CR Media
Sweet Spot	An instinct for opportunity and an eye for design

A broken wrist isn't usually considered a blessing, but for Chuck Reese the injury was just that. In addition to

---

10 For more on the Harlem jazz tour, check out www.bigapplejazz.com.

neglecting his academics, the Buffalo State basketball player had also been getting into trouble and hanging out with the wrong crowd—habits he'd picked up on the streets that he couldn't seem to break.

For Chuck, the injury forced a period of reflection, enabling him to reconsider the direction his life was taking. The skills he'd needed to survive a childhood of violence and drugs wouldn't be of use to him here, and would only serve to hold him back from the future he dreamed of. He knew from watching his friends where his current path would lead him—and the future looked grim. "This only ends in jail or death," he remembers thinking. He'd grown up in a world that constantly told him no. High school administrators insisted that college was beyond his reach. He met his biological father just once as a newborn—only to have the door slammed in his and his mother's faces. Chuck had always had to make do with harsh realities and limitations. Still, he was a natural-born entrepreneur who possessed an intelligent curiosity and a tenacity that had served him well on the court. He knew it was time to make a change.

It wasn't the first time Chuck had been forced to make a drastic life choice. In his teen years, Chuck's mother, who'd had him when she was just sixteen, sent him away from the negative influences of his neighborhood to live with an aunt in Richmond, Virginia. She refused to let him come home until he had "some sort of plan for his future." It was during countless games of basketball with his cousin that it first occurred to Chuck that he could get serious about basketball—a decision that led him to Monroe Community College, and two years with a basketball team that would go on to win a regional championship. He transferred to

Buffalo State University and continued to play, until his devastating wrist injury brought everything to a halt.

Unable to play basketball, Chuck felt another door slam in his face as he once again had to consider his next move. A teammate suggested he turn his hobby of always filming everything into a career by enrolling in a video-editing course. Chuck figured "maybe I could be the next Bryant Gumbel." He fell in love with the medium and transferred to the School of Communications, launching himself into the world of media and communications.

After graduation, Chuck found himself with no job options and only three hundred dollars to his name. His only lead, a friend's newly created video production company in Long Island City, New York, had been short-lived, despite his ability to sweet-talk his way into better projects. "That was the street side," he explained of his charm. "If you can hustle dope, you can hustle anything." Chuck quit after being asked to do one too many menial odd jobs. "I kept seeing people with laptop computers on set, and they seemed to be better dressed and be getting paid more than I was. I wanted to be one of them."

With nothing else on the horizon, he started working at a temp agency and found a job helping to coordinate training sessions in office buildings. He saved up for his own laptop and started learning software programs like PowerPoint, Excel, and Photoshop. He spent evenings and weekends in the aisles at bookstores, poring over books on graphic design software that he couldn't afford to buy. His next temp assignment would be the break he was waiting for: working with BBDO, one of the big ad agencies in New York, designing the slides for upcoming business pitches. He would spend his lunch hours honing his computer skills by painstakingly recreating the layouts from popular magazines and eventually put together a portfolio of work. It was during this time that Chuck realized he could make two to three times more money working directly for clients like BBDO instead of having to go through a temp agency. After a while, he didn't just design the presentations, he started reading them as well, and learned how to create a persuasive pitch, how to sell, how to market. Every new assignment was an education in the advertising industry, and Chuck took it all in. "I knew I could be more," he said. "I was seeing things that others weren't and I could communicate that."

Eventually, he left the temp agency to pursue the dream of building his own company. Today, Chuck has a thriving graphic arts business and counts companies like Sony Music, Ogilvy & Mather, and Columbia Records as clients. When he thinks about the kid he used to be, Chuck feels proud about everything he's accomplished. "You have to open doors for yourself. Always ask yourself, 'What's on the other side? Why can't I go there?' Never stop looking ahead and making yourself lucky."

Chuck Reese's career journey carries many rich lessons for the rest of us. His efforts in Stage One set the scene. I love how he was so resourceful in finding ways to learn. He absorbed valuable skills from school, sports, apprenticeships, and even nights scouring the bookshelves. Despite a tough environment and plenty of temptation, Chuck surrounded himself with good people, and invented an ecosystem to help propel his career forward. His resilience, chutzpah, and sheer tenacity meant that he never passed up an open door. One of his career highlights was the day that he was invited by the CEO of an ad agency to take one of the few available seats on the corporate jet to a multi-million dollar new business pitch. Reese was on that plane because he had made himself absolutely indispensable to the pitch's success. When asked about career low points, Chuck says: "I've never really had one. I'm always wondering about what can be and where I can go next."

Today, in Stage Two, Chuck is finding ways to scale up his business. He is sourcing a pool of talented young designers so that he can focus more on his own unique skills—winning new customers and providing the emotional guarantee that any work by CR Media will be 100 percent right. He is learning to trust others and to let go, without sacrificing the quality that got him where he is today.

As a Leader, What is Your Cruising Altitude?

Chuck Reese is not alone in wondering how to scale up his impact. One of the big concerns that people experience in Stage Two is how to transform from a doer to a leader. The approach that made them successful in Stage One often doesn't translate very well as they try to increase their impact without just working longer hours. The issue is "cruising altitude." Leaders must be able to fly high enough to be strategic and see the big picture. Any senior executive must be able to do this, because you are one of the very few, maybe the only one, who can see the whole picture. At the same time, effective leaders also require the ability to get extremely granular to solve a tough problem or close a deal.

The trick is to be able to alter your cruising altitude like a dive-bomber. You fly high in the air to survey the landscape and spot big problems or opportunities. Once you identify a target, you have the ability to home in on it and crush the objective. CEOs who have a serious crisis—like a mining disaster or a security breach—get right to the center of the issue and get their hands dirty and stay engaged until the mission is accomplished. But once it's done, you know when to fly back up again. We all know leaders who only have their heads in the clouds. We also know others who seem to operate a few inches off the ground, micromanaging and interfering. Don't just be a high-flying astronaut or a low-flying crop duster. One of the biggest challenges for rising leaders in Stage Two is to adjust from a command-and-control leadership style to an influencer style. Learn how to adjust your cruising altitude. Become a dive-bomber.

The full transition from doer to leader is more complex than just cruising altitude. It has a lot to do with attitude. Here is the advice I wrote in letter to a rising star in our company who had just been promoted to become the leader of one of our biggest offices.

Advice for a New Leader on Day One

1. Your presence, attitude, and demeanor are now highly visible and contagious. Staff will look to you like never before for signals on how well they are all doing. Whether you are expressing happiness, stress, confidence, cynicism, disappointment or danger, effective today the staff will pick up your signals and adjust their own attitudes and behaviors accordingly. Think hard about what signals you want to send.

2. Once you land on a vision, make it simple and repeat, repeat, repeat. It is so easy to overestimate the capacity of an organization to absorb vision and a rallying cry. Find a simple collection of words that expresses the basic direction you want the organization to go in. They need to be directionally correct and memorable, not perfect. Put "news" and changes in the context of your enduring beliefs and vision. "This is happening as a reflection of our deep belief that X is important." Repeat at every opportunity. You may think it's getting through, but it probably isn't. Remember that every year maybe 20 percent of staff turnover. Why should they remember last year?

3. Decide early who is on your bus. Every leader needs a small core team of close colleagues who can deliver on the agenda and the mission. Choosing this group is often a leader's most important task. You do not need to fill every seat right away, but you need to know who is on board with you early on. Do not choose people who are just like you. Find people who can complement your strengths and compensate for your weaknesses. Get to know the incumbents and the candidates one-on-one. Probe their ambitions, beliefs, and concerns. How do these fit with your own ambitions, beliefs, and concerns?

4. Every meaningful business issue is solved in a small quiet room with a few people. Confrontation is healthy. Make sure it is tackled in the right forum. Avoid repetitive flame e-mails. Contentious issues might best be confronted in smaller groups rather than big, acrimonious public meetings. Even though you're the boss, communicate *explicitly* that you understand other parties' points of view. Lead with your ears, not just your mouth. Probe the logic and consult your own beliefs. Then make a call.

5. Act like a trusted problem-solver, not a big boss. It's not the trappings of the office that are important, but your impact on the organization. Your conviction, integrity, and relentlessness will give you power. Share news in the organization transparently. Tell people the good news and the bad news, and provide a healthy perspective on what it means to the organization. Demonstrate that you are dedicated to the cause, you care, and you won't go away.

6. You don't know all the answers. Nobody does, and nobody ever did. It's wise to consult with others. It's okay to say you don't know, as long as you find out and make a decision. It's okay to make decisions that last for specific periods of time, not for eternity.

The person I gave this advice to has gone on to be a top star in our global company. He may not have taken all my counsel, but he has progressed tremendously as a leader and has a bright future ahead.

Sometimes, people in the prime of their careers find that they are running out of gas and need a change of pace or a change of venue. At age forty-four, Andrea Longueira found that her career had stalled. After almost twenty years in the TV broadcast business, Andrea felt she was getting pushed aside, or maybe even pushed out. A lot had changed with her employer, and the new people on the rise did not know her or appear to value her experience and skills. It was time to reassess her situation and what she wanted to do. Getting fired or retiring was not an option. She needed the money to provide for her family. Andrea took stock of her strengths—she knew the sports business, she was skilled at handling notoriously demanding celebrity talent, and was a hands-on and accountable operator. She started looking, both inside and outside her company. She seriously considered an opportunity inside her firm, but felt it was too close to what she had done in the past, and might be vulnerable to downsizing in the future. She needed something to stretch her and something that could keep her skill set fresh for the years ahead. In particular, she needed to make her skills as a producer relevant in a world gone digital. After a concerted search, Andrea found a new home. She now works as a production manager at The Players Tribune—a new online sports content platform backed by Derek Jeter. Andrea acknowledges that making a change wasn't easy after eighteen years in the same place. "My first day on the job, I had butterflies—like a kid going to a new school. But I really needed a push. I needed some urgency and also some confidence to get out there." The skills that Andrea possesses will be very complementary and valuable in her new workplace. In exchange, Andrea is learning everyday about how to apply and adapt her two decades of wisdom to the digital world. This will give her career a boost for years to come.

• • •

As you proceed through Stage Two, you should be constantly fine-tuning, and sometimes overhauling your career direction. Periodically, we need to make sure we're on the right path. Ask yourself those four critical career health questions we learned about back in chapter 5.

- Learning—Am I accumulating new skills, experiences and relationships to help me grow?
- Impact—Am I making a difference to individuals, to the company and perhaps even to society at large?
- Fun—Is my career generally a source of positive energy and joy in my life?
- Reward—Am I building economic value?

By the end of Stage Two, you want to be your best. Not all of us aspire to become CEOs, but it's interesting to hear what top recruiters look for when they recruit CEO-level executives. We can pick up some great clues on what top leaders do as they reach for the highest levels. I talked to two seasoned practitioners who have a combined forty-two years of experience with a leading global recruiting firm, placing thousands of top execs. When you boil it down, this is what they believe separates the best CEO candidates from the also-rans.

What the Experts Look for in CEO Candidates

1. Integrity and Fit. Top candidates exhibit strong personal values, and talk a lot about the potential fit between those values and the employer culture. Weaker candidates do not explore enough around "fit" between the organization and themselves.

2. Intellectual curiosity and agility. The best CEO prospects can synthesize and connect issues. They have an interesting and rich life outside of work. They read and are in touch with the world. They ask good questions. Poor candidates do not do enough research about the industry and the specific job opportunity. This is considered inexcusable and arrogant.

3. Track record of driving business performance ahead. This one is always tricky. The candidate's historical performance needs to be adjusted for the context of the industry and the situation. In some job roles, just keeping things steady is a big achievement. In some fast-growing industries, moderate growth will actually be below par. Recruiters need to tease out how much of the performance was inherited or circumstantial, and how much was actually the result of the candidate's contribution. The best candidates are able to articulate what the realistic goals were and how they delivered. One of the underlying factors that can drive CEO performance is "grit and self-control." Leaders who possess lots of grit (the ability to focus on single objectives through thick and thin) and self-control (the ability to resist distractions and temptations) consistently achieve better outcomes.[11]

4. Authenticity, self-awareness, and balance. It is okay to be vulnerable and imperfect. Good candidates have a clear-eyed view of what they've accomplished and draw lessons

---

11 See the work of A. L. Duckworth and others.

to improve things further. Not enough self-reflection on and learning from both successes and failures is a red flag. Too much "I" and not enough "team" make a candidate less attractive, not more.

5. Energy and passion. Top candidates let their passion shine through. If they are interested in an opportunity, they do not play coy—they show their enthusiasm. It makes people want to be a part of their team.

Stage Two: Reach High—Summary

Stage Two is the time to establish what makes you different and to back your strengths. Like "World's Greatest Salesperson" Todd Herman, we need to stake out our sweet spots and constantly hone them. Rachel Moore separated herself from the pack by finding a unique intersection of skills—the arts and business—that led her to the CEO chair. Is there an intersection you can occupy that will make you stand out? Chuck Reese took advantage of all that incredible groundwork in Stage One and created a powerful niche for himself as a small business owner. Now, like so many leaders, he is trying find a way to scale up his impact and find the right cruising altitude. Surround yourself with people who complete you and compensate for some of your shortcomings. Pour your energy into making your strengths even more powerful. Reach high.

As you move through Stage Two on your way to "reaching high," you will want to periodically check your progress. The four big career questions (Learning, Impact,

Fun, and Rewards) are a great start. You should also do the occasional career inventory exercise as we outlined in chapter 5. Are your fuel levels growing, shrinking, or staying the same? What is the quality of your career ecosystem? Is it expanding and creating deeper bonds, or withering and stagnating with old contacts? In the past year, have you been approached with new career development opportunities inside or outside your firm? If so, do they point you in the direction of your career ambition, or somewhere less relevant? If you asked important colleagues to describe your sweet spot, what would they say about you? How would you describe your career equity—the amount of positive energy and momentum you have in your career?

CHAPTER 10

Stage Three—Going Far

"At times our own light goes out and is rekindled by a spark from another person. Each of us has cause to think with deep gratitude of those who have lighted the flame within us." —Albert Schweitzer

The later stages of a career need not be a depressing slide into oblivion or a rude shock on retirement day. A well-planned Stage Three can be exceptionally long and deeply rewarding. The key point is to be relentlessly proactive about shaping the later stages of your career. Just letting things happen will not get you where you want to be. The world ahead will be littered with grumpy, late-career victims. Don't be one of them.

It's pretty obvious that people are living longer, but the speed and extent of the changes in longevity are breathtaking. According to the noted cultural anthropologist

Mary Catherine Bateson in her 2015 TEDx talk, in developed economies over the past century we have added thirty years to human life. As Bateson points out, it is not just longer "old age," but an entire extra stage of life before we get old.

For most of our lives, work is a source of fulfillment and happiness. For many people, the act of stopping work creates a true sense of loss—loss of identity, value, and feelings of contribution. Bateson sees ages fifty to eighty-five as a whole new era of opportunity. For the first time in human history we are seeing an entirely new age, where many people are both in decent health and experienced. Bateson encourages us to visualize ourselves as pioneers landing on a new continent. It is the age of "active wisdom." Lynda Gratton, author of *Shift* and *The 100-Year Life*, foresees careers lasting up to eighty years, punctuated by a diverse portfolio of career experiences and a lifetime of learning, doing, and teaching. By any standard, the later stages of a career are going to last for a very long time. Are you ready for a Stage Three that could last fifteen, twenty-five or even fifty years? As inspiration, let's meet Tim Penner.

Profile: Work Hard at Work Worth Doing

TIM PENNER
Age 60

Role	Senior advisor to companies and not-for-profit organizations
Sweet Spot	Business strategy and community causes

"I didn't want to be just known as the guy who sold more toilet paper than anyone else in the country," Tim Penner joked. Tim had spent over three decades at Procter & Gamble, eventually taking the helm as president of P&G Canada. But since stepping down as a leader of one of the top consumer packaged goods companies, he's also become known as the guy who raised hundreds of millions of dollars for his community and who helped raise the funds to build a major new facility for at-risk youth.

Many successful executives crash into retirement and find themselves bored, lost, or even depressed. Tim Penner wanted to make sure he wasn't one of them. Today he spends his retirement heavily involved in advisory roles, both in the for-profit and not-for-profit sectors. His for-profit boards include an insurance company, a retailer, and a coffee company. His charitable work includes serving, until very recently, as chair of the YMCA of Greater Toronto— he remains active on the board as a past chair. Tim is also a volunteer board member for a children's hospital and a healthcare innovation organization. He loves his advisory work as much as he loved his day job as an operating leader at P&G.

Tim joined P&G in the brand management division right out of business school because "they asked me better questions," and spent the next fifteen years steadily rising through the ranks. At thirty-seven, he wanted a bigger challenge and began taking on global assignments in the UK and in the United States, at P&G's headquarters in Cincinnati, Ohio, before returning for a triumphant twelve-year run as president of P&G's Canadian operations. (We'll take a closer look at his international career in chapter

12.) As a senior executive in Stage Two, Tim worked hard to balance seventy-hour workweeks with a full family life. Commenting on his rise through the ranks, Tim notes: "It never gets easier. If you're really good at something, they give you more responsibility and work, not less. It's not about conforming, it's about performing. Make your boss and your company successful. There is no substitute for putting in the hard work."

Tim's successful transition from Stage Two to Stage Three wasn't just a happy coincidence, but rather the result of several years of experimenting and planning. "In my early fifties, the big question for me was 'What's next?'" he said. "How do you follow that kind of professional intensity when you have thirty or even forty years of life expectancy ahead? I realized that it's not about walking away from something, but about being drawn to something different, a different purpose." Since he didn't have a precise idea of what he wanted to do next, Tim started experimenting with various roles and organizations outside of his responsibilities at P&G. He tried a volunteer board job at his alma mater, but found it frustrating. He worked with an industry association where he met some good people, but didn't fall in love with the work. "I needed to experiment a lot before I found my next mission," he recalled. "Even discovering what I didn't like was useful."

It wasn't until he worked on a big fundraising campaign for the United Way of Toronto, where he helped raise over $100 million for community activities, that Tim found the right fit. One of the organizations sponsored by the United Way was the YMCA of Greater Toronto. The YMCA combined two of Tim's greatest loves: kids and sports. "It turned out to be a perfect fit for me," he said. "I had learned things in business at P&G about raising support and money for your ideas and about how to fund capital projects, and could apply those skills here." In Tim's view, the YMCA was a true "doer" organization that built skills and character, and created opportunities for young people. He became deeply involved as a board member, heading up their fundraising efforts and later became the board chair of the YMCA in Greater Toronto once he'd officially retired from P&G at age fifty-five.

There are those who believe that transitioning from a for-profit career to the non-profit sector is somehow a step down. Tim disagrees. "People in the for-profit world often look at those in the non-profit sector and think they are less talented, possibly because they make less money," he said. "My experience is that people in the not-for-profit world are equally as talented as those in the for-profit sector. They just chose a career with rewards that are less monetary." He describes his experience in the non-profit sector as an opportunity to continue learning and growing. "There are some things they can learn from me, but I get more than I give."

Giving back has been a strong part of Tim's style as a leader, reflected in the high respect and bond he has built with his colleagues. Unlike senior leaders who can make people cry when they show up, Tim is one of those rare leaders whose teams always cry when he leaves. Tim's focus on helping others—whether it was his colleagues at P&G or through his volunteer work—created a richness in his working experiences that has made him a happier and better person. For him, retirement has given him the opportunity to devote more of his time to helping others, something he does happily. "Giving back feels good. I'm proud to have made a difference in improving the lives of those less fortunate in our community."

Tim has made the transition to Stage Three far better than most. He applied some thoughtful experimentation as he entered Stage Three, trying different roles to fit his new life stage and ambitions. Tim took stock of the skills from earlier stages that could still prove useful to a new organization. He successfully embraced the big mind shift that so many fail to grasp in their careers—going from "doer" to "advisor." Today in Stage Three and nominally retired, Tim still devotes at least thirty-five hours a week to work, but most of those hours are in community and not-for profit work. He credits his purposeful work and his daily fitness routine with keeping his energy levels high. Tim retains a healthy view towards growth and learning. "It's not about managing your career; it's about managing your learning curve. To make your learning curve steep, take on a tough problem and volunteer for challenges."

While for Tim Penner, not-for-profit work has become the main plank of his latter-stage career, for a growing list of others is it entrepreneurship.[12] Last year, over 25 percent of all new businesses in the USA were started by people over the age of fifty, up from 15 percent just twenty years ago.

---

12 For more on trends in entrepreneurship among those over fifty, consult the Small Business Administration and AARP.com.

Entrepreneurship opens up a vast new field of opportunity for people in Stage Three. The risks are real, but the rewards can be immense. Meet Sue Piper.

Profile: From a Company of 400,000 to a Company of One

SUE PIPER
Age: 50s

Role	Founder and president of Silk Road Boutique in New York
Sweet Spot	Adapting and evolving

When Sue Piper traveled to India, she was so inspired by her experiences that she came back to New York and launched a new business, a retail store specializing in textile goods from the East. There are many people who find their next business idea during their travels abroad, but not many who would choose to jump into a brand-new career after they had already retired.

Sue graduated from Vassar College, and was a part of the first coeducational class of the formerly women-only college. "Computer Science was still in its pre-formative stages, and I didn't think I had the personality or temperament for sales, so I chose psychology."

Sue joined the ranks at IBM after realizing her first job after graduation, a position with the Irving Trust Company, wasn't exactly what she'd expected. "I hated the commute and hated the job, so I stuck it out for a month or two before

I quit," she recalled. "I joined IBM as a typical junior trainee and over the years rotated through different human resources positions. It seemed like a natural fit with my degree."

She enjoyed the challenges of her role at IBM, and took advantage of all the professional development programs they had to offer to continuously improve her skill set. "IBM always has been and continues to make sure its employees grow. I had exposure to some fabulous training programs that allowed me to develop new skill sets and better myself," she said, never expecting that she would end up staying at the same company for thirty years. "It just kind of happened."

It wasn't all rosy. The company that employs over 400,000 people experienced some rough patches. "I went through some very tough times at IBM in the 80s," Sue recalled. "That was when there was the first consolidation, then the deconsolidation. There were a lot of layoffs, plant closures. The company survived and prospered, but having worked there for thirty years I feel like I worked for three different companies, it changed so much every decade."

Closing in on her third decade at IBM, she realized that she was no longer as engaged in her work as she'd been in the past and decided it was time to move on. "I realized I had plateaued and that probably partly led to my decision to leave, although I did wait until I reached that magical thirty-year mark," she said. "I do have a defined pension." Sue didn't want to stop working completely, and so began to do some freelance projects and consulting that kept her employed for a few more years.

At fifty-two, she was invited to accompany a local college on a trip to India. It was on this trip that she and her soon-to-be business partner Janet would share a love for the colorful tapestries, textiles, and art they saw during their trip. Sue spotted an opportunity to bring some of these goods back to the West.

Upon their return, the two women decided to join forces and start a retail store called East India Designs, though neither of them had any previous retail experience. Initially, they had hoped to target interior designers who were looking to secure one-of-a-kind, high-end pieces for their clients. They found a small space on the outskirts of the local business district. The store opened its doors in early 2008, which unfortunately coincided with the beginning of the now-famous recession.

Their business model wasn't working out the way they had anticipated, and their location didn't bring in enough foot traffic. "My time at IBM had taught me that when something wasn't working, I should just try something else," Sue explained. They experimented with several different approaches, including hosting wine and cheese soirees to attract customers to the store, using direct mail campaigns, coupons, and implementing e-commerce aggregators like Shoptiques. They decided to change their location, their target audience, their merchandising—and even their name. They launched the newly rebranded Silk Road, which focused on lower priced goods targeted at a broader audience.

A pending spousal relocation for Janet prompted her to leave the venture. For Sue, the dissolution of their partnership jeopardized the future of the entire store. "I seriously thought that was it," she admitted. "I didn't know what to do next, and there had been big financial and time investments. It was pretty tough." It would be a defining moment for Sue, who would have to reassess her commitment to the project.

She realized she wasn't ready to walk away, and so took on a risk by taking out a bank loan to help carry the store alone.

"I made the decision that I would redouble my involvement in the store," Sue said. "I've seen too many absentee store owners. I've also been lucky that I've always had incredibly talented women working with me." She does wish she had some more experience with retail before she decided to launch her own business, but admits her time at IBM helped to equip her nonetheless. "The notion of being flexible, being innovative, thinking outside of the box, and embracing the Internet as much as possible are all things I learned during my time in HR," she explained. "Reflecting on everything I've learned, even in my little one-person enterprise, I still use some of the training and exercises." Sue experiments constantly, trying different merchandising approaches and sales channels. She actively seeks the advice of experts inside and outside the world of retail.

Today, Silk Road enjoys a growing clientele, and was named Best Home Furnishings and Gift Retailer in her home county. The revenue continues to grow steadily, but it is not the money that Sue finds so rewarding. Silk Road has become an established part of the local community. It is place where teenagers buy their Mother's Day presents, guests buy hostess gifts, and local brides register for their bridal showers. Silk Road hires students for part-time work and has become a launchpad for women returning to the workplace. Even local pets feel welcome at Silk Road. Sue has beaten the odds and has passed the eight-year mark in business. It's been challenging, but worth it. "Entrepreneurs need to be passionate about what they do," she advises. "It's too hard otherwise. Without the commitment, they won't survive."

How Will You Invest in You?

I hear constantly from friends and colleagues who are retired or considering retirement: "How will I fill my days?" Remembering the personal time portfolio exercise from chapter 6, it's actually a very strategic question.

One day about four years ago my wonderful, creative colleague Jan Leth came into my office to talk about "his future plans." He put a rough pie-chart drawing down on my desk with the following details:

- Fishing: 32%
- Painting: 17%
- Kayaking: 20%
- Gardening: 21%
- Consulting for Brian: up to 10%

After almost forty years of intense, full-time work, this was Jan's way of saying he was moving to Maine in about six months and beginning a new chapter of his life. I was delighted to see that he had left a small sliver of his talent available to me, but it was a bold statement about how Jan wanted to spend the next phase of his life and career. I respect the fact that it was purposeful and thoughtful and proactive. Jan has pretty much stuck to his time portfolio over the past four years, though I do confess that the 10 percent can occasionally go higher, just never during fishing season.

Not everyone is so proactive in how they will spend their time in retirement. Is retirement really the time to extinguish the flame and turn out the lights? Some people I talk to give me the impression that their new time portfolio for retirement looks something like this:

- Work: 0%
- Community: 0%
- Grandchildren: 10%
- Golf: 90%

I adore golf, but it is not a full-time avocation unless you are a PGA Tour phenom. A few people are wired to gear down to a life of golf and beach walks, but most of us are not. The prospect of hitting the wall on retirement day and packing it in is pretty daunting, and as it turns out, may also be unhealthy. A friend of mine shared this quote, from a therapist who counsels people approaching retirement: "In a car, if you are traveling at seventy miles per hour and you stop dead, you are going to go through the windshield. The same is true in careers and life."

At age sixty-four, fitness buff and long-time retail executive Jim Bunn was feeling very healthy, but conflicted about his career future. "Should I wrap it up, or do one more big gig?" He'd had a long and varied career, starting in retail and becoming a senior executive in the fashion, cosmetics, and fragrance businesses. One of his career highlights included running the $500 million Calvin Klein business for the Americas. When Calvin sold the company, Jim got into consulting, and then pursued a series of entrepreneurial ventures around his sweet spot of fashion and retail. Jim's last corporate job was as global CMO of a luggage company. The firm wildly miscalculated its global ambitions and financial forecasts. Jim found himself out of work and was very uncertain about what to do next. He and his wife Jackie sold their family home and experienced a classic "what now?" moment. Should Jim pursue one more corporate thing, or another entrepreneurial venture, or after more than forty years of work, maybe it was just time for him to chill? As it turns out, Jim found a career gem and launched his next chapter right in his home community. Today, Jim is vice president of Institutional Advancement at Concordia College, a liberal arts school outside of New York City, which serves a diverse population of about a thousand students from thirty-five countries.

Before he took the job, Jim worried that maybe the educational not-for-profit sector wasn't for him. He also didn't want to just dabble or do it half-heartedly, treating the job like a refuge. Jim's kids intervened, saying, "It's perfect for you Dad. You just have to do it." Jim committed to it as a serious next chapter, and can now see a pathway to perhaps even seventy years of age. Jim says his new job draws upon every major career experience to date: retailer, brand marketer, internationalist, CEO, and Sunday school teacher. Jim spent the first few months understanding the mission and purpose, relentlessly asking questions like: Why do people work here? Why do students go here? Why should people give money to support what we do? Jim says he won't leave until he gets real results. His previous chapter ended in failure, for reasons beyond Jim's control. He will not permit that to be his final career legacy. As Jim declares: "I will retire, but I am going to do it on my own terms, with a feeling of contribution and a smile on my face, not because some other exec blew his global forecast."

Here is what research tells us about people's reasons for retiring. Among younger people (age twenty-one to thirty-five), there is a strong belief that it will be prompted by "hitting a number" on how much wealth they have accumulated. By age fifty-five, there is a more balanced view of the reasons for retiring. Money is less decisive, and health reasons come to the fore.

Most Important Factor on Decision When to Retire (The Futures Company 2015 USA. n= 1,644)				
	Age: 21–35	Age: 36–55	Age: 55+	TOTAL
Reach certain age	21%	23%	28%	23%
Accumulated enough financial resources	52%	44%	25%	43%
Health or mental capacity begin to fail	19%	21%	27%	22%

In my experience, there are a number of events that tend to trigger serious retirement planning. It could be a traumatic event like a medical problem or the death of a loved one. Some people get put on notice by their employer or offered a package. Some hit a milestone birthday. Some start waiting out the clock until they simply cannot take another day. A few do retirement planning as a healthy and purposeful part of life. The best advice I have heard is to be really wary of stopping cold—only a few people seem capable of really doing that well. For most of us, it seems best to dial it down, not turn it off. And finally, "leave while the music is still playing"—before you lose all the joy and respect you have built up over the previous years.

Stage Three: Go Far—Summary

How will you approach Stage Three? Will you be a victim, or an agent of purpose and active wisdom? Start thinking ahead well before you hit the wall. Create a plan to pass the torch of your expertise and mastery to the next generation. As Lloyd Blankfein, CEO of Goldman Sachs, said recently: "People owe mentorship to the next generation. You are not smarter, just older. They are not dumber or less worthy, just younger. Young people are entitled to have their questions answered." Get ready to compete for purposeful work, even if you are willing to do it for free. I love the concept of "active wisdom," but for people who want to thrive in Stage Three, it comes with responsibilities. First, you need to have developed some real expertise and mastery in earlier career stages. People don't just want your opinions or descriptions of how things used to be. They want true depth. Second, they want something that is relevant to the present and the future. Part of "active wisdom" is to stay fresh.

Sir Martin Sorrell, seventy-one, runs WPP, the world's largest communications company with over 190,000 employees worldwide. He is legendary for responding to hundreds of e-mails every day, almost never more than thirty minutes after receiving them. Sir Martin knows every major development in the exploding world of digital technology. How on earth does Martin Sorrell stay on top of it all? His strategy is to talk to customers, fellow CEOs, and rising stars every day. For the past ten years he has hosted the global series of conferences called WPP Stream, bringing together tech leaders from around the world to share and debate the latest issues. I think staying current is a critical job for people in later stages of their career. What are you doing every day to contemporize your skills and your context? I am taking my own medicine on this topic. My chosen field of advertising and marketing is already a dog-eat-dog world.

It is aggressive, and it is a young person's game. In the digital marketing sector where I specialize, the youth factor is even more acute. For the past decade, I have very often been the only person in the room with grey hair. I could easily have drifted into oblivion or thrown in the towel years ago. What I have tried to do instead is stay fresh. I go into the study cave and do my homework on emerging topics like mobile commerce and marketing automation. Once I know my material well enough, I write articles and make speeches. I actively seek out reverse mentorship. At least twice a week, I consult with teams of rising stars in our company—offering advice but at least as often seeking perspective from their end of the telescope. I use LinkedIn and mentorship platforms like Ten Thousand Coffees to provide counsel, but also to hear youthful voices on hot topics. If you are entering or immersed in Stage Three, what is your plan to keep learning and stay fresh?

Stage Three doesn't have to be a bummer—it can be awesome. Lay the tracks for your next stage before retirement is upon you by building a healthy arsenal of transportable skills. Take a clear-eyed view of your strengths and your passions. Be willing to study and experiment before you find your next love. Reset your expectations. Become a part of the "active wisdom economy." The pay might not be the same as when you were in your prime, but there are great career chapters that offer you other powerful rewards—applause, respect, personal accomplishment, and the feeling that you are making a difference. Enjoy the deep satisfaction of passing the torch and lighting a new flame.

3

CAREERS AND
REAL LIFE

CHAPTER 11

Careers and Parenthood

Parenthood is a momentous life event that can occur in Stage One, Stage Two, or even Stage Three of a career. Yet after years of debate and reform, many working people still fear that parenthood will negatively affect their careers. Too often, employers assume that parenthood somehow signals a lack of commitment to a career. This issue now affects not only women but also men. It is a huge issue for business, which faces acute shortages of the right kind of talent. How can we expect to overlook or underleverage vast pools of talent and still fuel the innovation and economic prosperity that the world needs?

Janet Kestin and Nancy Vonk are mothers, authors, and executives who succeeded in a notoriously demanding and inhospitable job role—as creative directors of an advertising agency. Half of the employees in the advertising industry are women, but only about 5 percent of creative directors are female. Both Nancy and Janet rose up through the ranks of advertising and then shared the top creative role at Ogilvy & Mather in Toronto. They became one of the most awarded creative partners in the industry and led their people to multiple Grand Prix awards at the Cannes Lions advertising festival. Today, Janet and Nancy run a creative consultancy called Swim, devoted to teaching leadership and creativity to the next generation. The duo has authored two best-selling books, *Pick Me* and *Darling, You Can't Do Both (And Other Noise To Ignore On Your Way Up)*, the latter of which tackles the issues of motherhood and careers head-on.

For Janet and Nancy, the ride wasn't easy. As Nancy says: "For years, career women got no advice on how to manage kids and job. Women were afraid to have children, especially early on, before they felt their careers were secure. Everybody worried about it, and nobody knew the answers. Having kids was interpreted at work as a lack of commitment. Men assumed that you were getting off the 'up' escalator— and many women were equally as dismissive."

Janet adds: "For many of us, career and motherhood were pitched as an either-or decision. High-performance cultures seemed to demand that you be all-in, all the time, and the belief was that children took you out—if you were a woman. My son was born before I had much of a career, and as far as I can tell, motherhood made me better at my job. As more men start to want the quality of relationship with their kids that women tend to have, everyone needs to be asking, 'Why should having children come with a judgment as to how well people will do their jobs?'"

Janet and Nancy are optimistic about the potential for future progress. They cite the enlightened policies coming out of Scandinavia, and feel that as men now look to spend more time with their children and families, it will help force change. As Janet notes: "The happy kids of happy working parents will be the gift that keeps on giving."

One of the few jobs more brutal on family life than advertising creative director is to be the CEO of a lean start-up. Milena Berry and Paul Berry both run their own successful start-ups and are raising three kids together. How do they do it?

Milena came to New York City from her native Bulgaria at an interesting time—just one week before the terrorist attacks of 9/11. Despite no formal background in art, she was able to talk her way into the prestigious Interactive Telecommunications Program at New York University and was taken under the wing of Red Burns, the legendary teacher and "godmother of Silicon Alley." In Milena's words, Red taught her "to embrace change, to never fear what's next, and to act out of inspiration."

Milena worked for seven years in technology, becoming a full-time CTO with three kids. She found it very challenging. Milena got a frantic call from a friend of hers one day. "The bus is leaving. Where are you?" Milena had totally missed a school field trip. The pain and strain of Milena's work-life balance came to a head at the moment her daughter Eva (then six years old) asked: "Mommy, why are you so unhappy about your job? Why do you keep doing it?"

For Milena, the joy of work was dimming and wasn't worth the pain. Milena and a friend decided to start a new company called PowerToFly, a professional women's networking platform that connects women in technology with jobs they can do remotely. "Imagine the growth in societies when you enable women to work," she says. "I really want to enable companies' growth and access to talent."

Many organizational cultures favor long work hours that can be unsustainable for women who have children to take care of, and which often leads to missing out on promotions, raises, or career-advancing projects. Forced to make a choice between family and work, many women step away from great careers in favor of spending more time with their families, a decision that Milena believes they shouldn't be penalized for. She wanted to create a company that connected women with great career opportunities that also provide a satisfying work-life balance. "The challenge of raising children and being a full-time professional applies to women all over America, not just the big cities," Milena explained. "If you live in rural North Carolina, it might just be a lack of economic opportunities all together."

Remote work provides a solution that tackles both geographical proximity and work-life flexibility while enabling women to keep investing in their own professional development. PowerToFly eschews the traditional office politics associated with "face time" culture for a flexible approach that focuses on output and performance, instead of the time spent in the office. "I'm a big proponent of remote work. All of our talent comes to us because they want to work in this way and for me, it's how you can achieve work-life balance," she explains. PowerToFly brings together talented women and tech companies who are willing to have employees work remotely. It's not for everybody, but it opens up a huge pool of talent.

Milena's husband, Paul Berry, is the CEO of Rebel Mouse, a publishing platform for distributed web content, and is also a big supporter of new ways of working. "I don't count people's hours," he said. "You can't pretend that every hour of the working day you're on. Some days you're off. If so, then go home or take a walk. It's not about the amount of work you do or the total hours you put in." Paul actively challenges routine face-to-face meetings. When he does meet staff at work, he almost always makes it a walking meeting. He finds it more productive and energizing. He is a big fan of crisp, decisive e-mails. "I like a culture that can make decisions. But is this meeting really necessary? There's a difference between need-to-have and nice-to-have."

Milena and Paul know that demanding full-time jobs and a demanding family life can take their toll. Stress is contagious. Says Paul: "Stressed parents can transfer it to their kids. With a consuming job like running a start-up, there are so many highs and lows." That's one of the reasons that the Berrys set clear boundaries for family time so that they can establish some space and calmness in their lives. From 6:00 p.m. to 9:00 p.m. they focus solely on their children. No work phone calls or e-mail. The family dedicates an hour each evening to reading books together. Despite both parents being in the tech business, the Berry children go virtually device-free. No smart phones, no TV. Kindles are OK for reading time, but when the Berrys travel, the preferred distraction is paper and crayons, not an iPad.

• • •

Janet, Nancy, Milena, and Paul have thought hard about how to make parenthood and career work together. Here's my summary of their collective wisdom:

1. Don't make careers and parenthood an either-or decision. Don't be afraid to have a baby because it will necessarily jeopardize your career. Those who have succeeded in pursuing both point to the growing list of work-family options. And if parenthood means a temporary step away from the full-time workforce, it need not be permanent.

2. Find a family-friendly employer. They are out there. Industries and employers vary wildly in their degree of flexibility and hospitality. Ask people on the inside what it's really like on the ground. Consult the "best places for working parents" listings. Here's an announcement my own company, Ogilvy & Mather just made regarding an enhanced parental leave policy in North America:

> Returning to work after a parental leave can be a stressful event. There are many lifestyle adjustments required and decisions to be made. It is hoped that easing back into the work environment through a transitional leave will help both you and your manager to accommodate the new responsibilities of your home life and the ongoing responsibilities of your job. Transitional leave provides that the primary caregiver will be able to return to work on a part-time basis (minimum of twenty hours per week), for up to twelve weeks. During this transition period, your salary will be adjusted accordingly. You will be required to discuss the

schedule with your manager as soon as you can before returning to work to ensure that all needs can be met as much as possible.

Policies like this seem smart and fair.

You may also find that certain countries are more receptive to working parents.

Scandinavia now has parental leave for both mothers and fathers. To smooth transitions, part of parental leave is now devoted to orderly handoffs between the outgoing parent and the less senior employee who will step up to do their duties. This is framed as a great learning opportunity. Parenthood is now a normal part of work life, not a painful experience for the employer and coworkers.

Some industries and jobs simply have structural barriers—like constant travel and chronically unpredictable hours that make parenthood an extreme challenge. Some jobs just don't work. As one working mother puts it: "You cannot simply wish the constraints away."

Even if your industry, employer, or country is generally receptive, you will also need individuals at work who will actively support you. Janet and Nancy had each other as work partners, and were able to divide and conquer on specific tasks or at crunch times. They were not "job-sharing"; they were both doing huge jobs. But being there for each other got them through many potential crises. Who will back you in a moment of truth?

3. You cannot survive without a proper support system at home. The experts agree that you cannot make it work without an effective support system on the home front as well. Choosing your "system" will be a very personal decision.

Support could come from a spouse, partner, family member, daycare, babysitting service, nanny, or some combination of options. Milena Berry says that even if you are trying to work remotely from home, you need support to get you through critical moments like mornings and back-from-school time. A working mother who ran a 20,000-person company once said: "Your nanny might be the most important employee in your life. You can't pay them too much or say thank you too often. If the home fire is not well tended, work will suffer."

4. Set realistic expectations and firm boundaries. Do not set yourself up for failure and unhappiness. Pitching yourself as "the workhorse" who will do anything at any time on any schedule may not be a realistic positioning for you. Saying yes all the time can be a recipe for disaster. You need to become a master of the "conditional yes." Make it clear that you are wildly capable, enthusiastic, and committed to the team's success. You can be flexible, but there are limits.

I once went to an astonishing event at the United Nations. It was to honor my boss at the time, Shelly Lazarus. Shelly was an accomplished global CEO, a board member, inspiring speaker, and industry leader. She's also the mother of three kids, and the event was to recognize her as Working Mother of the Year.

The event could easily have just recounted her prodigious career accomplishments and tossed in some passing platitudes about family life. Instead, the person giving Shelly the award did an amazing thing. He read out her performance appraisal—from her children. It was thorough, candid, and poignant. Each of her children—Ted, Sam, and Ben—commented on the appreciation they had for her as an industry leader, but also as a mom. As they grew to understand what she did for a day job, they marveled more and more at how she set boundaries to enable her to be there for them, from simple family meals to big moments of truth.

I know for a fact how hard some of these boundaries were to keep in place. When Shelly became the Ogilvy leader on the global American Express account, expectations were high. She was revered, and often seen by the clients as utterly indispensable. When American Express invited her to an all-day five-year planning session, Shelly let them know that she would not be arriving until 1:00 p.m., because she had already made an important commitment to one of her children. She was willing to do extra prep beforehand, and extra follow-up that evening if necessary. At precisely 1:00 p.m., Shelly entered the conference room, accompanied by a few raised eyebrows from the other attendees. As Shelly explained: "If I wasn't there in that conference room for a couple of hours, nobody was really going to miss me. But I just couldn't back out on my son's school field day. Shelly continues: "You can't be there for them all the time. You may be away from your kids for days at a time on business. What's important is that they are secure in the knowledge that they are the most important thing in your life. It's not the hours. It's the feeling."

Shelly does not believe that setting boundaries means you need to keep family and work life totally separate. From the time they were little, Shelly's kids were included in the conversation. Shelly would share some of what happened at work, and occasionally bring them along for office visits or business trips. Once, Shelly's work and family life almost became irrevocably intertwined. The very first time I met Shelly, I was a young upstart at Ogilvy Canada. We were pitching together for a global assignment from American Express on their new Optima Card. Shelly was eight and a half months pregnant at the time. In a moment of high theater, she promised the clients that if Ogilvy were awarded the business, she would name her child Optima. We didn't win the assignment, and I am delighted to report that her son is now called Ben, not Optima.

The most effective boundary-setters are good at communicating where the open capacity is and where the friction spots are. "Yes, that is a great assignment, and I can do it Tuesday, Thursday, or Friday, but not at noon on Saturday." If it is important to avoid the "unconditional yes," it is also essential to avoid the "unexplained no." When working parents turn down tasks or jobs or promotions, others *assume* that they are inflexible and no longer interested in progressing. You need to *explicitly* take this thinking off the table. A female executive I know was offered a huge promotion, but knew that at that moment she could not balance it with her family commitments. Instead of just saying no, here is what she said. "I think that is a great job, and I could do it exceptionally well. But at this particular moment I have family commitments that are extremely important to me, and I would not be able to do the job the way I know it needs to be done. I am grateful for the offer. I remain serious about my career here and I want to find more ways to contribute in years ahead. This job and this moment are not right for me, but keep me in mind for the future." To me, this was a great way to manage expectations and to keep her decision in proper context of a forty-year career:

this was a temporary and worthy pause, not a terminal career move. That woman is now the president of a multi-billion division of the same company.

5. Manage your time and your energy. Janet Kestin talks about working parenthood as the ultimate way to hone your time management skills. "When I first started, getting help or asking for help was a sign of weakness. I learned to ask for help and delegate as a survival skill. Avoid mindless doing. Showing up at 9:30 a.m. clearheaded and refreshed might be better than showing up at 9:00 stressed and muddled. It is not about hours, it is about outcomes." When it comes to productivity, Milena Berry talks about the "sacred three." "You've got to get three things right in order to manage your stress levels and cope with things in life: sleep, diet, and exercise. Those are the three things that no one can do for you, that you have to do for yourself because those are what keep you going." Milena cannot function without them and she's willing to sacrifice the number of work hours for the quality of work hours.

Coming Back After an Absence

Sometimes, regardless of your coping strategies, parenthood may take you completely out of the workforce for a period of time. Since you still could have decades of your career left, this should not be a terminal state. Yet thousands of workers, especially women, find it immensely challenging to get back onto the career track. As a society, we have not made the transition easy, and as a result millions of highly skilled workers have never returned to work. There is hope. Meet Laura Harrison.

Profile: A Lot of Employers Offer Internships. What About "Returnships?"

LAURA HARRISON
Age: Late forties

Role	Program manager in a technology services company, mother of three kids
Sweet Spot	Knowing how to get back into the game

Laura Harrison knows the exact moment she decided to leave the full-time workforce after almost two decades working with tech giants like IBM and Sun Microsystems.

"It was four o'clock in the morning. My eighteen-month-old son had severe asthma and was throwing up in his crib. I calmed him down and he crawled into bed bedside me while the two older girls slept nearby. My husband was out of town on business, and I knew there was no way I was going to work the next day. I just asked myself, 'What am I doing here?' and drafted a resignation letter on the spot." A few days later, Laura officially resigned and stepped away from full-time work to focus on family.

After a few years, Laura started up some volunteer work and tried some substitute teaching. She worked briefly in another tech firm, and then experienced what so many boomers face—the sandwich generation effect of simultaneously caring for kids and aging parents. "After a point, I knew I wanted to get back into something full time. But how, and where? I worried that my skills were rusty. And I feared that in the tech space, so much of what I had learned would be obsolete. Everybody in tech kept talking about the 'agile method' and I had grown up with an approach called 'waterfall.' I had some skills, but how could I learn about the new tools and find a place to fit in again?

"I heard about this thing called 'returnship' from a friend who worked at Return Path, a technology services company. The whole idea is to give experienced managers a chance to reactivate their careers in technology after a period away from the workforce."

Laura applied, and was one of six women who earned a returnship position. The program matches up new "returnees" with managers in the company who need experienced talent and are willing to invest some time in training and development. It starts with an eight-week technical skill-building curriculum. As Laura notes: "I had some good skills, like time management and executing multiple projects, but I was so unfamiliar with a lot of the technologies that millennials take for granted." The functional technical training is supplemented with support around the softer skills like leadership, teamwork, and collaboration. The class of returnees receives group training from the HR department, and spends frequent one-on-one sessions with their assigned bosses. One of the most important sources of support comes from the six returnees themselves. As Laura describes it: "The company kitchen became our haven. It was a safe place to talk among people who shared so much. We could talk about the little stuff, the big stuff, and the really tough work-balance issues: the juggle and the struggle." At the end of the twenty-week program, five of the first six candidates were offered full-time or contract work at Return Path. The program is now in its fifth cycle and is being expanded rapidly. The latest cohort has almost forty participants across six locations.

The returnship program at Return Path was proposed by its chief technology officer, Andy Sautins, and then quickly embraced by its CEO, Matt Blumberg. Matt started up Return Path on a simple premise. Some start-ups are designed with a very "shareholders first" approach, intended to maximize the financial return on investment. Other companies are built on a more enlightened "customers first" approach on the assumption that this will create more lasting value. Matt's approach is different. He has chosen deliberately to pursue a "talent first" approach on the deep belief that customers and shareholder returns will follow. "My deal is simple," says Matt. "I offer employees freedom and flexibility in exchange for high performance and accountability." So far, it has worked spectacularly. His company is now home to over five hundred employees in New York, Colorado, and eleven other offices around the world. In a company whose whole existence depends on the quality and motivation of its staff, Matt is always looking for rich new talent pools to keep the company growing. He found an irresistible one: career women who had stepped away from the full-time job market to have kids. According to Matt, the early results are outstanding. "Our company gets access to a phenomenal and under-utilized talent pool. Returning employees are highly productive, and are proving to be deeply loyal to the firm." Matt is currently expanding the initiative into a 501c3 charitable foundation called Path Forward to make it easier for other companies to access the curriculum and the learning.

Laura is grateful to Return Path for setting up the initial program she enrolled in. "I love technology and I'm good at it, but I just didn't know how to get back into it. Return Path provided the curriculum and the culture. People met in the kitchen just like a family." She continues: "I am optimistic about my career. I love work and want to do something for a long time to come."

I have seen a lot of successful and some unsuccessful returns. To me, there are four essential ingredients:

1. Refresh your skills. If your skills are rusty or irrelevant, you need to deal with it. Perhaps you will become one of the lucky ones to join a returnship apprentice program like at Return Path. If not, find other ways to rejuvenate and contemporize your skills. Take courses from an adult school, university, community college, online curriculum, or an innovative source like General Assembly. Do volunteer projects. Talk to people who are currently in the industry (not just the old vets you may know best). Create a two-way mentorship or skills exchange with a young person: "I'll teach you this if you teach me that." Embrace the challenge. Set short-term goals, like, "In the next thirty days I'm going to learn how to build a simple website for myself." Start somewhere simple, and rebuild momentum off small victories.

2. Reframe your experience. You have lots of great experience, but if you are returning after a considerable period, it will often be expressed in dated terms and contexts. Some aspiring returnees I have met spend the entire interview name-dropping or babbling about long-ago war stories. They talk about their past, and only bring up the future to dismiss it ("this crazy digital stuff") or say how they don't understand it. Why on earth would an employer spend precious pennies hiring that candidate? You must reframe what you know and link it squarely to the present *and* the future. Study the future vision of the industry you are trying to reenter. Subscribe to current industry publications and blogs. Put your skills, wisdom, and experience squarely in the context of the employer and where they are heading. Your past is only relevant to the extent that it will help your potential employer succeed. They don't need to hear war stories about how you and your cronies invented the Internet in 1997. Tell them what you know and what you can do that will help them succeed today, and over the next few years.

Do your homework on the industry. Read speeches by the CEO. Find out what the industry analysts are saying. Read the annual financial reports that are available for every public company online. Even if you are not a financial wizard, you will get to see how the company talks about itself and its future.

The language you use as you pursue your return will be important. What used to be called X is now Y. A lot of times, the principles are highly similar, but if you get the language wrong, you sound like a dinosaur. Last year, I talked to a super-talented woman who was trying to reenter the marketing world. The language of 2005 (direct marketing, digital media, websites, targeted television) had been replaced by a whole new lexicon (performance marketing, programmatic media buying, distributed social platforms, mobile video content, etc.), and every time she opened her mouth she became less employable. She needed a serious refresher course in the new language of her chosen field. By doing some homework and talking to some veterans who were also relevant in the new world, she was able to translate and update her experience into contemporary language. Employers began to see her as a wise contributor rather than a geek from the past.

Once you've updated your knowledge of the category and the firm and its language, figure out the story of how you fit in. Write it down. Polish it and bulletproof it. Hone it into a crisp two-minute introduction. Rehearse it.

> So, here's my story. I worked for _____ years and became a world-class expert in _____ and _____ (Include one or two points of compelling evidence). I have been out of the workplace for X years in order to _____. What I really want to do now is _____. I have done extensive homework on the future of your industry and your firm. It is exciting to me because _____. I want to be part of it and feel I could bring _____ and _____ that would help you succeed.

Now, that person might be of serious interest to me. At least I want to hear them out and give them a shot.

3. Reconnect your career ecosystem. If you have been out of the workforce for more than a couple of years, I guarantee you that your career ecosystem will need a serious overhaul. Dropping the names of ex-colleagues and retired execs doesn't help you. Take a look at all major elements of your career ecosystem (see chapter 5)—your connections, communities of experts, critical colleagues, and champions. Get on LinkedIn, Facebook, and any other social networks that can bring you closer to relationships that are relevant to your industry. Reactivate your alumni associations. Join industry groups. Plan on drinking dozens, if not hundreds, of cups of coffee.

4. Reboot your self-confidence. Successful returnees constantly refer to the need to rebuild their self-confidence. As one working mother jokes, her self-confidence was understandably low after spending a decade talking to kids who have double-digit IQs. I have heard this comment a thousand times, and have actually invented a tongue-in-cheek mathematical hypothesis called "Fetherstonhaugh's Theory of Fixed Household IQ."

It goes something like this. Two adults with perfectly reasonable IQs enter a relationship and begin living together. Together, they create a combined household IQ score. Unfortunately, my mathematical theory suggests that the total household IQ is fixed, regardless of the number of people in it. So, as kids come along and grow smarter, they absorb more of the household's "fixed" number of IQ points. The parents inevitably get dumber and dumber. As the kids progress in age and number, they suck up more and more IQ points, leaving fewer and fewer IQ points for the parents. By the time the kids are teenagers, the parents are dumb as posts, and richly deserve constant eye rolling for their low IQs and bad judgment. When kids leave the household, the parents magically start to recover their IQ points. After the kids are gone, parents report extraordinary events—like kids actively seeking their advice, and willingly spending time in their company. Hundreds of empty-nester parents I know report the same phenomenon. (I haven't worked it out completely, but I think that adults get stupider around grandchildren, too. Let me know if you have worked out the math.)

The theory of fixed household IQ is a bit of a joke, but the issue of confidence is deadly serious. In their book *The Confidence Code*, Katty Kay and Claire Shipman present evidence suggesting that women tend to have too little self-confidence. When asked how well they did on tests, women tend to estimate that they got fewer answers correct than they actually did. In one British study, a business school professor asked students how much they would deserve to earn five years after graduation. The women's estimates were 20 percent lower than the men's. Spending several years out of the workforce does little to increase the base levels of confidence. An extraordinary woman I know is a graduate of two Ivy League schools. In her late forties and facing an impending divorce, she sought to re-enter the workforce after nearly fifteen years away from full-time employment. I was struck and touched by the disconnection between her exceptional skills and her low confidence level when she first went back to work. At first, she was really worried about the cool factor—everybody in her new company seemed so young and hip. She was anxious that her methods and her tech knowledge—even the presentation software package that she used—marked her as an oldster. Would she ever fit in? After an angst-ridden start, she started surrounding herself with eager young minds and together they embraced a form of two-way mentorship. She learned about new techniques and technology. But she also discovered that the new generation really appreciated her substance and wisdom. "I can do valuable things that these young hip people actually cannot. I learn from them; they learn from me." This woman has now become president of a global consulting operation and an inspiration for the next generation of returnees.

I think that returnships are a huge idea. I do not think that they should just be a program in one or a few pioneering companies. Returnships deserve to be a global movement.

Careers and Parenthood—Summary

It will be a crime if employers and employees cannot figure out how to stop making careers and parenthood feel like an either-or decision. Employers are too hungry for the right talent, and parents are too hungry for the right kind of work. Organizations need to create more flexible and enlightened policies for working parents. In the meantime, career-oriented parents need to create strategies and take action, including: finding parent-friendly employers, identifying the support system at home that works for you, learning to set boundaries, and managing your time and energy. "Returnships" should become a global phenomenon, built around the principles of reframing past experience, refreshing skill sets, reconnecting career ecosystems, and rebooting self-confidence. The payoff for getting the career-parenthood equation right will be immense: productivity gains, increased innovation, and happier lives.

CHAPTER 12

Going Global

"Wherever you go, go with all your heart."
—Confucius

The desire to travel the world shows up consistently as one of people's top life goals. Interestingly, it is not just for the young dreamers or the old folks with plenty of time on their hands. It is a top-rated goal across all age groups and almost all countries.[13] Most of us would love to visit, but how many are willing to work in a foreign country? In a world where an increasing number of career paths present both global opportunities and global competition, how do you decide when, where, and how to take an international job? What are the benefits, realities, and pitfalls of accepting a post outside your home market? Meet Karl Moore.

13 The Futures Company Global Monitor, 2015.

Profile: Oh, The Places You Will Go

DR. KARL MOORE
Age 59

Role	Associate professor at McGill MBA School, and author
Sweet Spot	Academics, industry, and international experience

During a flight from Zurich to Kuala Lumpur, Karl Moore calculated that he'd visited forty-one countries in his forty years, a realization that sparked an ambition to always visit more countries than his age. Now fifty-nine years old, his mission has been successful so far—he has over sixty country stamps in his passport and plans to add Myanmar and Rwanda next. It's to be expected, of course—Karl is a professor at McGill's MBA School in Montreal, and a worldwide authority on globalization.

His own career is a prime example of the increasing accessibility of international markets. Karl grew up in Toronto, Canada and pursued his undergraduate studies in California. He worked in systems engineering at IBM and global product management with Hitachi. After completing his PhD thesis on global industries, he spent five years in Europe teaching in England, Holland, France, and Finland. He also spent three years living in Tokyo. He decided to return to McGill University to work alongside one of the world's leading experts on management—Dr. Henry Mintzberg.

In 2006, Karl hit upon a great idea. He took twenty McGill management students on a pilgrimage to Omaha,

Nebraska to learn from legendary investment guru Warren Buffet. The event would transform into a recurring series called "Hot Cities of The World," where students would apply for the opportunity to accompany Karl on intense learning visits to burgeoning global markets such as Bangalore, Doha, Jakarta, and Moscow. "It's like taking the future to the future," Karl explained.

He believes that global experience is an essential part of today's career development. "In the past, you competed with students and workers from your home country," he said. "Today, you compete with the world—for jobs and for customers. That's why it's so important to experience other parts of the world, especially the high-growth, high-innovation markets."

A global mindset is a very transportable skill, as it creates an appreciation for a diversity of thought and culture. It can help open doors and lead to new experiences. Stepping outside of one's comfort zone can be an enriching and meaningful experience regardless of your career ambitions. Karl encourages his students and graduates to experience global markets as much as possible. "Learn by living and visiting. Engage with families," he advises. "Sometimes it will be difficult or impossible to learn their language. Don't give up. Read about the country's history, geography, and culture. You have no idea how much people appreciate it when you make the effort to learn a little about their history, their heroes, and their music."

Global experience makes you more interesting both personally and professionally. "You can talk to more people and it's a great conversation starter when students go to job interviews," Karl says. One of the best times to "go global" is during one's twenties and early thirties. People are often single, or have very young families that might be easier to relocate. "International assignments are a great way to build a base of skills in the early years, at a time when you have some freedom to experiment and explore. Check out different industries, roles, and countries."

Karl's own background proves the validity of his approach. Global experience has been a key differentiator in his career. He is a sought-after expert due to his unique combination of in-depth academic authority, his practical working experience with recognized industry leaders, and his first-hand understanding of various countries—an expertise he's methodically built over several decades. As Karl recommends, "Know something substantial about at least two continents—your home and one other. Those who thrive in their roles will be the ones who have deliberately chosen to expand their horizons by going out and discovering all the world has to offer."

Someone who clearly embraces the global challenge is Justin Cruanes. Justin joined Karl Moore on the McGill Hot Cities expedition to the Middle East a few years ago. The trip whetted Justin's appetite for global adventure, but he wanted to go deeper and work right at the epicenter of global enterprise. I spoke to Justin via Skype from his temporary accommodations in Burundi, Africa.

Profile: Seeing The Emerging World Up Close and Personal

JUSTIN CRUANES
Age 26

Role	Business operations associate for One Acre Fund in Burundi, an NGO operating in East Africa
Sweet Spot	Economic development in the emerging world

Justin was born in the US and grew up both there and in France, and studied economics and finance at McGill University.

Always an adventurer on a mission, Justin spent two summers working in Syria helping to set up a school for illiterate factory workers. His plan to find a permanent job in Syria in 2011 was foiled by the Arab Spring uprising. As plan B, Justin moved to Rabat, Morocco and landed an internship with a USAID contracting company working on improving local governance. He then moved on to Terre des Hommes, a Swiss NGO focused on child protection. Justin says, "I loved the early responsibility. As a twenty-four-year-old, I had eighteen staff reporting to me across three organizations." After a year, he contemplated his next step, wondering whether to focus on humanitarian aid, economic development, or the private sector.

Justin found a really good job about a year ago. He is now on a two-year contract with the One Acre Fund NGO. As Justin explains, "It's a social enterprise that provides agricultural products such as seeds, fertilizer, trees, solar lamps, and stoves on credit to local farmers, along with training. The idea is to help farmers in Burundi, Rwanda, Kenya, and Tanzania grow beans, potatoes, and hybrid maize in order to build economic self-sufficiency."

Justin really respects the One Acre Fund organization and its "farmers first" philosophy.

He likes the social mission and the travel to unique, less-travelled places. He likes how an organization like One Acre Fund gives him such responsibility and opportunity for social impact.

His bosses and peers are smart people. His boss is a Northwestern MBA, highly consultative and supportive. Justin gets a proper development plan, with goals and performance feedback at least every six months.

In Burundi, Justin dives deeply into the local community. He lives one hour outside the capital, in a village with fewer than 6,000 people. The daily menu is rice, beans, and cabbage. Justin cooks for himself. He has learned from hard experience that you do *not* go to the local hospital. If you are really sick, you have to go to Nairobi or the Gulf Coast. Electricity and water supply are spotty; both sometimes go out for one-to-two-week periods. Internet is available sporadically via satellite. Justin was amazed that our Internet Skype session worked for over thirty minutes without interruption.

Justin acknowledges that the short-term economic rewards are low, but the cost of living is so low that he is financially self-sufficient. As Justin reports, "I save much more than many of my colleagues who now live in New York, London, or Paris." He also believes that the long-term economic rewards will be good. "I am learning from world-class people, getting early responsibility, and gaining first-hand exposure to entrepreneurship in fast-growing markets."

Like so many people doing less conventional things, many said to Justin, "You must be crazy." He grew up in the French education system, where so many strive to get a Masters degree. Many told him, "Go do a real job." Most people do not consider NGO jobs to be a serious career. His father, an entrepreneur in the US and France, was encouraging. "Do something interesting with your life—not just pure business."

Justin says: "I want to link business and purpose. For me, that is first prize." Justin's advice to others seeking serious global career adventure: "Get out there. You cannot find an interesting international assignment from home. Move to the region. Get local. Network. Make it easy for someone to say yes to you."

In his career to date, Justin has done a lot of discovery. Looking ahead, he is contemplating whether he should do another one or two international NGO assignments—something like North Africa, the Middle East, or South America. Should he do a Masters in public administration or business? Should he stay in non-profit or migrate into the private sector for something like consulting or global banking? He is a bit worried that if he stays in the NGO world too long, he will be pigeon-holed as a "not for profit" worker, and doors will be closed to him down the road. Justin sees himself possibly working in a major global development organization like the World Bank or International Monetary Fund, or perhaps working in a global consulting firm that needs help in economic development in emerging markets.

Justin's global experience is more extreme than most, but it underscores the core benefits of international career development. By getting outside his comfort zone, Justin has been given incredible early-career exposure. He is wise and lucky to have worked with organizations that offer not just hardship but also top-class training and feedback. He has found work that is challenging and meaningful. He has used his hands-on international assignments to build skills and differentiation into his career. As a result, he has a range of diverse and career options.

Back in chapter 10 on Stage Three careers, we met Tim Penner, the former president of P&G Canada who found new purpose and joy after retirement by becoming a community leader. A big part of Tim's career experience has involved international assignments, both good and bad.

Tim's international experience began at the age of thirty-seven. He was steadily climbing the ranks at P&G Canada, but starting to look for something more. "The company was expanding internationally and it looked like a good pathway forward." So Tim and his wife Pat decided to move their young family to the UK. Tim went on to have a tremendous run there, leading the turnaround of the struggling P&G UK Health & Beauty Care business. "International assignments are great because they take you out of your comfort zone. More than anything else, you learn to depend on your own team, because you just don't have your usual network and connections." It turned out to be a fantastic experience both career-wise and personally. Tim and his team turned around their P&G division, to the envy of others. "It's not a bad thing to inherit a mess, a piece of crap. It forces you to learn and stretch. You figure out who to trust. There is a risk you will flame out, so you learn to be all in." Tim's next move was to P&G's headquarters in Cincinnati, USA. For Tim, it was much less rewarding. He missed the accountability and freedom he enjoyed in his earlier roles. He found that his political radar didn't work as well.

After three unhappy years at HQ, Tim expressed a strong interest in going back to Canada. When the company restructured its North American operations, Tim made a pitch to return to Canada. He hungered for the autonomy and impact of the world outside of HQ, and wanted to put down roots in his home country. It turned out to be a highly successful move for P&G, and for Tim. He was able to leverage all the learning he'd accumulated around the world, and reinvigorated a team at P&G Canada that was languishing. Together, Tim and his team built an enviable track record over a twelve-year period.

Tim has some wise reflections on global experience. "In contemplating an international assignment, the key is that you and your whole family need to treat it as an *adventure*. When you can't find the breakfast cereal your kids liked at home, or the hobbies you like, or the sports you watch, the whole family has to recognize it as part of the adventure. You need to all be of a mindset that says, 'I wonder what the kids here eat for breakfast,' and then relish the opportunity to go learn and try it out. If you can't go into the experience ready to relish the new adventure, then you shouldn't go international at all. That adventure brought us closer together as a family and was a source of much laughter, not tears."

Tim spent a total of thirty years with P&G and rejects the notion that staying in one firm necessarily limits your learning. "I have had hundreds of people tell me that staying with just one company is a mistake. It simply isn't always true. The important thing is that you find somewhere where you can learn and grow—where you can open doors. From the time I was twenty-two till I was fifty, I had an incredible learning curve inside my company. Since then, the steepest learning has come from the outside." Tim continues: "Don't close any doors until you're forty-five. Before making a career decision always ask: 'Will this open or close doors for me?' A lot of my peers left too early for bigger titles or bigger money. But often these moves closed doors instead of opening them. Working for a second-rate company closes doors. Look within your organization first."

What if your life circumstances won't allow you to do a full-time international move? What are other, more practical options on the spectrum? Consider working domestically, but in the division of your company that handles international customers. Apply for a short-term assignment to fill an international job opening for a few months. Take courses that introduce you to global topics. Do a special project that gets you involved in analyzing international business—sizing up foreign competitors coming into your home country, or perhaps helping your own organization decide if it should expand internationally. Volunteer for (or offer to create) an international training program that matches you with someone in another country. Let your bosses know that an international assignment is part of your longer-term career ambitions. Make sure that your message gets through to the senior ranks, because international assignments are often outside the domain of mid-level executives.

Going Global—Summary

When I think about Karl, Justin, Tim, and my own global experiences, I am convinced that international exposure must be at least one pillar of a modern career. It adds diversity, robustness, differentiation, and refreshment to the long slog. Spencer Stuart recently reported that nearly three-quarters of chief executives had worked internationally or oversaw a global function. Their average shareholder return was far higher than CEOs without this background.[14]

There are no guarantees that an international assignment will be successful or smooth or deliver a perfect financial return. Some people worry that they will get "off the radar" by taking on an international role. In my experience, the reverse is usually true. Carrying the badge of international experience gives you more profile, not less. What is critical, though, is that you have a champion in both the sending and receiving markets. International transfers can be rocky and stressful. Get expert advice (ideally though your company) on issues like tax rates, foreign exchange, and visa requirements. These can often become a major stressor if you make the wrong assumptions. Make a conscious effort to leverage your career ecosystem so that you have someone championing your cause from both ends. Going to a "small market" from HQ gives you an appreciation for how to get things done with fewer resources. Making the pilgrimage from a smaller market to HQ gives you respect for how to navigate complex issues on a bigger scale. Having the right mind-set is critical. Global assignments must be viewed as an adventure—by you and any family members along for the ride.

---

14 Research by Spencer Stuart as reported in "More CEO Jobs Go To Inside Candidates," *Wall Street Journal*, March 9, 2016.

CHAPTER 13

Overcoming Adversity

"Everyone has a plan, till they get
punched in the mouth." —Mike Tyson,
former heavyweight boxing champion

The one thing I can guarantee about your career is that at
some point you will face adversity. You will get laid off. Or
fired. Or passed over for a raise or promotion. Or stalled,
or forced into retirement. Adversity is a normal and healthy
part of any long-term career. It is how you react to adversity
that matters.

Your first step when facing career adversity is to take a
clear-eyed view of the problem. Is it an unavoidable event, a
perception problem, or a performance problem? If it's truly
an unavoidable event or just bad luck (say, your company

unexpectedly got sold), move on as quickly as you can. It is okay to grieve or vent briefly, but the best medicine is to get back on your feet and into the game. Wrap things up with dignity, diligence and grace. Move forward.

Sometimes, a career setback will be caused by a misperception of your skills, ambitions, or performance. Perhaps your new boss doesn't know about your full set of skills or your stellar past contributions. Perhaps your firm doesn't know that you aspire to a new or higher position, and just passed you over. Perhaps you have been unfairly tainted with a performance issue that wasn't actually your own doing. Don't criticize the boss or the organization for failing to see your genius. Just take it on as a project and demonstrate your real value. If your product is actually good, you just need to build a better relationship. Find out what the perceived shortfall was and make it clear that the real you is better than the perception.

In many other cases, your shortfalls may not just be perceived, but real. If your clear-eyed analysis indicates that your actual skills and performance aren't up to par, you need to tackle the problem head-on. Find out what a good competitive level of skill and performance looks like—and work towards it. You cannot run away from problems. If someone got promoted over you, it is okay to quietly find out the skills that made the difference in the decision. Build the fuel that will make you eligible for the next raise, promotion, or juicy new assignment.

Some career setbacks can be anticipated and avoided. By thinking ahead and staying aware of what's going on in your company, your industry, and your own performance, you can often avoid getting blindsided. If you see that your industry, your company, or your job role is in danger, you need to take proactive action to give yourself a plan B. Build skills and relationships to inoculate yourself against the risks and give yourself options outside of your current situation.

Whether your career setback is unexpected or foreseeable, you will need a method to speed your recovery. The four Rs method mentioned in chapter 11 in the context of returnships is a good general approach to getting back on track quickly. If you get fired or pushed to the side, build on the four Rs to help get you back on the right path.

> **Reframe** your experience so that it connects to the future, not just to the past.

> **Refresh** any skills that are rusty or lacking. You cannot fake your way to renewed career momentum.

> **Reconnect** your career ecosystem. Maybe you need some fresh relationships with contacts, experts, critical colleagues and champions to propel you forward.

> **Reboot** your confidence. Talk to people who know you and get you. Reflect on the strengths and special contributions you have built over the years. Be brave.

Dr. Jules Goddard, author and professor at the London Business School, has one other piece of valuable advice: When facing a serious career crisis, get back in touch with humanity. Goddard works extensively with mid-career executives, many of whom feel anxious or downright fearful about the careers. He notes that age forty-five is often the low point of human happiness and that crises are common. His advice to those facing a serious crisis at any age is to change your attitude and quite possibly your latitude. Get out of your comfort zone. Spend some time on the dark side of town. Travel. Break out of rituals that can often hold you back. Even spending a day working at a soup kitchen could do you a world of good. Put yourself in a bigger context and get in touch with what's really important. Rediscovering your humanity will remind you of your blessings and how you can make a difference.

Jules Goddard and I agree that one of the biggest barriers to career recovery is pride. Healthy confidence is good. Bravado, denial, and wishful thinking are destructive. Fragility is the result of overprotectiveness. Adversity and stress are healthy. Goddard notes that in the weightlessness of space, we stop stressing our bones, and they become brittle. Your sense of confidence needs to be informed by what it means to be competitive in the marketplace. You will often have to step sideways or backwards to move forwards. When struck with a career crisis, park your pride. It gets in the way.

Nilofer Merchant is a woman who faced serious adversity at multiple points of her life and career, always ending up on her feet and moving forward. Meet Nilofer Merchant.

Profile: Staying True to You

NILOFER MERCHANT
Age 47

Role	Author, consultant, and speaker
Sweet Spot	Turning adversity into success

At eighteen years old, Nilofer Merchant came home to find her relatives celebrating having found a suitable candidate for her arranged marriage. She was only concerned with one thing. "I asked my uncle if he'd told the man that I wanted to go to college, but he said that my mother wouldn't let him say anything," Nilofer recalled. "My mother was a respiratory therapist, but she didn't value education for women." Being denied access to the very thing that had secured her mother's self-sufficiency was a frustrating contradiction, and the subject became such a contentious issue between them that Nilofer walked out of her house, telling her mother she would refuse the marriage suit unless her soon-to-be groom agreed to let her go to college.

"I threw a couple of books and clothes in a bag—a purely theatrical gesture. I walked down to a local coffee shop to wait for the call from my mother telling me she had reconsidered. I thought the whole thing would blow over in a couple of hours." But that call never came. "I highly underestimated how stubborn my mom is—and how stubborn I am." When neither woman backed down, Nilofer realized she couldn't go back home. With only a hundred dollars in her pocket, she spent the night at a friend's house while she figured out what to do. The separation turned out to be permanent—Nilofer remains estranged from her mother. She found a room, and landed a part-time job. "I ate a lot of ramen because you could get twenty boxes for a buck," she recalled. "I just pieced it all together."

It's very hard to reconcile the image of a scared young teenager with the confident and polished woman that Nilofer has become today. Now in her late forties, Nilofer has had an impressive career. She's worked for major companies like

Apple and Autodesk, and has personally been responsible for the launch of more than a hundred products, netting $18 billion in sales. Nilofer is also the author of two critically acclaimed business books and has been recognized by Thinkers50 as the number one person most likely to influence the future of management. She's happily married, and is currently living in Paris with her husband Curt and ten-year-old son, Andrew.

Nilofer started as an administrative assistant at Apple, a position she got through a temp agency thanks to a recommendation from a high school friend. It was a lucky break: her boss gave her the leeway to work on other initiatives even though they were beyond her official job description. Engaged and eager to learn, Nilofer jumped at the chance to gain more experience and exposure. "I basically raised my hand for every project they needed help on," she said, and described how she worked diligently to acquire the skill sets needed to tackle an ever-mounting list of projects, gaining a reputation as someone with a solid work ethic. "I worked ridiculously long hours to learn how to do new things. I'd take on extra work even if it meant working really late into the night. I kept getting different and higher level projects, and the teams around me appreciated my initiative so they would coach me through it." Despite her challenging workload, Nilofer upheld her commitment to continue her own education, taking part-time courses towards an applied economics degree from the University of San Francisco and an MBA from Santa Clara University.

Nilofer credits her upwards trajectory at Apple to her "say yes attitude" and her willingness to take on new challenges. One of those "yes" moments was agreeing to work on a project that no one else inside the company wanted—a struggling product line with declining profits. That project gave Nilofer the chance to not only manage her own team as product lead, but turn a $2 million product line into a $180 million revenue generator—a feat that earned her company-wide recognition and media attention.

Ready for a new challenge, Nilofer spent some time with a small startup called GoLive before joining Autodesk, where at twenty-nine she was managing a division worth $300 million. The success would come at a price. "I failed in a really political way at Autodesk," she admitted. "In hindsight, I didn't have the maturity. I had hubris. I'd been successful so I thought I was badass, and now I was willing to step on people to get ahead. It turns out that's not the best way to advance your career."

Grappling with her failure at Autodesk, and needing a break from the politics of the corporate world, Nilofer decided to start her own consulting company, where over the next eleven years she would build a first-class roster of clients that included Logitech, Symantec, and Hewlett-Packard, among others. Having a thriving business came with a cost: she was spending more and more time away from her family, and her son was starting to have some trouble at school and needed her attention. Despite trying several alternatives, Nilofer realized she needed to step away from the business and focus on her family. Walking away from the business she'd spent over a decade building was a difficult decision that obliterated her self-confidence. "I really felt like an incredible failure in my life at that moment," she recalled. "I thought that I was done, professionally."

For the first time, Nilofer felt lost, rudderless.

Transitioning to writing happened almost by accident. "I was sitting around in my pajamas—nowhere to go, no one to impress—and I was writing. I wrote several pieces that were about the future of business. Eventually they would become the foundation of my first book." *The New How: Creating Business Solutions Through Collaborative Strategy* would go on to become a bestseller.

It doesn't escape Nilofer that some of her most successful career accomplishments have emerged from events in her life she would have categorized as failures: leaving Autodesk led to starting a successful business, and closing down that business led to a new career as an author and speaker. These experiences have taught her to gracefully embrace periods of change despite their tumultuous nature. "In my twenties, I never thought I'd get there. In my thirties, I thought 'What the hell am I doing?'" she recalled. "If I could go back and tell my younger self something I would say, 'Girlfriend, don't stress so much. Stop worrying about everything else and just enjoy what you're doing.'"

Nilofer's trials and tribulations show how we can all struggle with our authentic selves throughout our careers. Nilofer was never one to back down from adversity, and after many successes and failures has found a great sweet spot as an author and consultant. She used the stress and adversity to build up her immune system. She learned from each setback. Nilofer also took accountability for her own behavior, recognizing when her actions were more detrimental than helpful and taking the necessary steps to rectify the situation.

• • •

The world of sports gives us stories of career triumphs, but also of massive risks and failure. How would you react if you were hit by a career thunderbolt? What if someone came to you in your early thirties and told you that you could never again do the work you were best at and most loved to do? Someone who knows this phenomenon well is Anthony Rodriguez, who works everyday with pro athletes.

Profile: Starting Over Before Age Thirty-Five?

ANTHONY RODRIGUEZ
Age 33

Role	Cofounder of Lineage Interactive, and advisor to pro athletes
Sweet Spot	Counseling athletes on the brutal reality of early, early retirement

"I'm personally very intrigued by the psychology of what happens in an athlete's last season," says Anthony Rodriguez, CEO and cofounder of Lineage Interactive, a firm that helps celebrities, mostly athletes and musicians, develop their brands and careers both on and off the field and stage. "Many of them have to find a new career in their early thirties, most likely in an area where they have no skills."

The reality is that most professional athletes have fast paced, compressed careers that are also notoriously brief. To put this into perspective, consider that the average playing career in the National Hockey League is 5.5 years. In the NBA it's 4.8 years, and that number drops to 3.5 years if you're in the NFL.[15] "No one's really written about what most athletes experience during their last season," Anthony points out. "In the professional world most people go through that stage when they are sixty to sixty-five, after they've experienced a long career."

Anthony has spent the last ten years of his career helping basketball, hockey, golf, tennis, and football pro athletes make the transition. It's a job that requires highlighting a difficult truth, even if it means telling a client something they don't want to hear. Many celebrities and athletes are surrounded by yes-men who are too afraid of being fired to tell the truth. Anthony takes the opposite approach, and insists on being brutally honest. He recognizes that his clients will have to make a difficult choice. "Most athletes will have to choose what to do with the next thirty years of their potential work life, but there's a giant catch: it can't be the one thing they've been doing since they were about ten years old," Anthony explained. "They can't go back to plan A."

Professional athletes commonly devote the majority of their time honing their performance, and many other skills and activities such as socializing, hobbies, money, and business management are neglected. For Anthony, helping his clients rediscover their passions and areas of interest is a crucial first step. "The simple exercise that I encourage people to do when trying to find their sweet spot is to look for three things: What are you good at? What do you love? What does the world need?"

While the first two are straightforward, Anthony insists

---

15 See Jeff Nelson, "The Longest Professional Sports Careers," *The Roosevelts.* July 22, 2013, www.rsvlts.com/2013/07/22/longest-sports-careers/.

it's the last question—what does the world need?—that holds it all together, creating the necessary conviction required to endure hardships and setbacks. "If you miss that third one you're always going to be frustrated, especially if you've become accustomed to the tangible rewards received from a career that you can no longer participate in. A few athletes have made enough money in their early years to be secure for life. Many athletes don't make a good transition, too used to the big income and lifestyle that often includes indiscriminate spending. After agent fees, taxes, and other expenses, there is often less money than anticipated." Sadly, many professional athletes end up broke, depressed, and unemployed. According to the *New York Times*, an estimated 60 percent of NBA players face bankruptcy within five years of leaving the court, and for NFL players that time shrinks to just two years.[16]

But some do it right. A shining example of a successful career and life after the playing days were over is Allan Houston. Houston was a star college player with the University of Tennessee before being drafted in the first round to play in the NBA with the Detroit Pistons. Allan went on to star for the New York Knicks, earning a reputation as a strong team player and one of the most accurate shooters in team history. In his early thirties, Houston suffered a series of injuries that hampered and then ended his career. By age thirty-four, his playing days were over. Says Houston, "My leg just couldn't handle it any more. I started playing less and

---

16 See Jonathan Abrams, "N.B.A. Players Make Their Way Back to College," *New York Times*, October 5, 2009, www.nytimes.com/2009/10/06/sports/basketball/06nba.html?_r=0.

less, and after a while, I decided I couldn't go on. I didn't want my body to be ineffective for the rest of my life."

But rather than fading into the pages of "Where Are They Now?" Allan Houston has thrived—as a manager, entrepreneur, and community leader. He landed on his feet right after retirement, serving briefly as a global ambassador for the NBA. Using skills he learned as a player in the spotlight of New York media, Allan also worked as an analyst with the ESPN sports network. After about a year, Donnie Walsh, then the general manager of the New York Knicks, approached Allan with an intriguing offer: to come to the Knicks organization to study sports management. Allan put his impressive curiosity to work. "I always seek advice from people I respect." He observed, studied, and asked questions. "There is so much to learn about scouting, operations, and management that you simply don't learn on the court." Allan has progressed to become General Manager of the Westchester Knicks development team and Assistant General Manager of the New York Knicks NBA team.

As Allan advanced, he learned more and more about the value of relationships. Throughout his life and career, Allan's father has been a central figure. The lessons Allan learned about being transparent and direct were critical to his later success as a manager and leader. Houston learned to "treat people with respect—even when the message is hard to deliver and hard to hear." When I asked him what was the most difficult aspect of his management role, Houston replied: "Trades and firings. Giving bad news to people who have such big aspirations and dreams. That's the hardest part."

Allan observes that young players today face even more

stress than previous generations. "The process that younger players go through is different. There is so much information and it's so quick. Young players see some immediate results, and think they are closer (to stardom) than they actually are. Expectations are so high. The younger guys today need patience, to respect authority and instruction. They need to trust the process. Just because you have information doesn't mean you have wisdom."

Allan's own wisdom seems to extend far beyond the sports world and into his whole life. In addition to a sports management career, his life embraces his deep faith, his wife and seven children, several entrepreneurial ventures, and a foundation that celebrates fatherhood. When asked about how he manages all his commitments, Allan explains that personal discipline and core values get him through the week and help him decide how to spend his time. Allan lives by a credo of faith, integrity, sacrifice, leadership, and legacy, backed by some practical lessons. On leadership, Houston notes: "You can express leadership in so many different ways. You don't always have to be the team captain. Be really clear about your role. You don't have to do everything yourself." Allan is grateful that his wife and family are so supportive. But he also knows he needs to set boundaries. "I'm learning to say no. There are some things that I need to do, and some that others can lead. I have also cut down on travel as much as possible."

Houston is deeply passionate about the topic of fatherhood and has created the Legacy Foundation to celebrate it. "My father was such a powerful figure. Not just as a basketball coach. Being his son is an honor." Through his foundation, Allan wants to share the joys and knowledge of his own experiences. "So many young men need to be trained in what manhood and fatherhood is." His advice to young men who didn't have strong fathers in their lives: "There's always someone there if you look hard enough. Nobody has it all figured out. There's always someone to help take you the next step."

As Allan sums up his own early retirement crisis and the journey that followed, he offers the following advice: "Figure out what you're called to do. What do you love? It might not be clear at first. Find places where your talents and passions can be used to have impact on the world. Set yourself on some kind of journey. It is okay to be uncomfortable. It's not supposed to be comfortable. Be willing to endure the hardships to do something you are committed to. Find mentors. Live your life based on a set of core values."

Almost none of us will be virtually penniless and homeless at age eighteen like Nilofer Merchant, or be forced to face retirement in our thirties like Allan Houston, but there is much to learn about how to triumph over career adversity. Use the weapons of curiosity and discovery to build up your immune system with skills and experiences that can ward off the inevitable setbacks you will face. Constantly seek your purpose and get back in touch with humanity if you have lost sight of what is important. Make sure that your confidence is well informed, and if your failures are the result of more than bad luck, take action to address the relationships or the skills that are lacking. Don't let pride get in the way of a successful recovery. You may need to go backwards to go forwards. Stay true to your core values and to your authentic self.

CHAPTER 14

The Future of Careers

"My interest is in the future because I am
going to spend the rest of my life there."
—Charles Kettering, inventor

"Happiness is an inside job." —William Arthur Ward

Since careers last so long and are so deeply embedded in our lives, when we talk about the future of careers we need to grapple with some pretty cosmic questions:

- Will I be replaced by a machine?
- Where and how will I find work in the future?
- What will I do with my time?
- Will I outlive my money?
- How will work make me happier?

Will I Be Replaced By a Machine?

On a sunny day last summer, I spend an amazing day at IBM's Thomas J. Watson Research Center in Yorktown Heights, New York. The Watson lab is home to some of the world's most advanced work on cognitive computing and artificial intelligence. I saw a demo of what machines could do, including a film featuring ELI, a robot that learns to recognize, choose, and move objects. The robot answers to voice commands and responds in English. It says when it knows what to do, and when it is confused. Eventually, after some trial and error, it makes all the right decisions. The possibilities are both thrilling, and chilling. If you are taking a really long-term view of careers, you need to ask yourself an awkward question. Over the next ten, twenty, or forty years, will my job be done by a machine?

There is no question that the machines are getting smarter. For example, in the past, computers have always had a tough time decoding natural human language, which is full of nuances and ambiguities. When we say the word "bat," which bat do we mean—the bat that flies around, the bat used in baseball or cricket, or the bat of an eye? Powered by algorithmic software and high-speed servers, IBM's patented Watson technology can read millions of documents in seconds and assess the context of what we say. Unlike its predecessors in the machine world, Watson has become a master of natural human language. It knows almost instantly exactly which "bat" we mean. In 2011, Watson beat the world's two best human players of the *Jeopardy!* quiz show.

Today, Watson is working in harmony with humans, in diverse fields such as the research and development departments of big companies such as Procter & Gamble and Coca-Cola—helping them find new products. As Adam Bogue of Watson Labs says: "It's not about man versus machine, but about a new symbiotic relationship between humans and machines." Watson is also being used in a dozen US hospitals, helping oncologists find treatments for cancer. It has even been incorporated into a toy dinosaur, allowing children their first taste of communication with an AI. They can ask the dinosaur questions, and Watson will help it answer them.

A recent report by the BBC (in September of 2015) puts the man versus machine debate in the forefront. "The debate about whether machines will eliminate the need for human employment is no longer just academic. Boston Consulting Group predicts that by 2025, up to a quarter of jobs will be replaced by either smart software or robots, while a study from Oxford University has suggested that 35 percent of existing UK jobs are at risk of automation in the next twenty years." The report goes on to review some of the 282 occupations analyzed in the Oxford research to assess the risk of replacement. Many of the most vulnerable jobs were mechanical and repeatable in nature. Office workers who do repetitive jobs such as writing reports or drawing up spreadsheets are easily replaced with software. Factory workers were becoming increasingly vulnerable as machines with better manual dexterity are developed. "As more advanced industrial robots gain improved senses and the ability to make more coordinated finger and hand movements to manipulate and assemble objects, they will be able to perform a wider range of increasingly complex manual tasks. However, manipulation in unstructured environments—like the tasks that must be performed by a house cleaner—are still beyond the scope of automation for the foreseeable future."[17] Interestingly, while taxi drivers are protesting against competition from Uber, their real competition may be coming from driverless cars. Driverless cars aren't coming soon—they are already here. A man drove his Tesla across America a few months ago, 90 percent of the time in "driverless" mode. Last week, the bass player in my weekend rock band drove his Tesla on autopilot to band practice.

By contrast, if repeatable and programmable tasks are on the decline, roles requiring employees to think on their feet and come up with creative and original ideas hold a significant advantage in the face of automation. This can be good news for artists, designers, or engineers. Additionally, occupations involving tasks that require a high degree of social intelligence and negotiating skills, like managerial positions, are considerably less at risk from machines according to the study. I was encouraged to see that my own role of CEO had a low risk of replacement, at 9 percent— not that I'm planning to be at my desk in 2035.

Claire Cain Miller writes in the *New York Times* (October 18, 2015), "Skills like cooperation, flexibility, and empathy have become increasingly vital in modern-day work. Occupations that require strong social skills have grown much more than others since 1980, according to new research. And the only occupations that have shown consistent wage growth since 2000 require both cognitive and social skills....

---

17 For more on Robots and jobs at risk, see "Will a robot take your job?", BBC News, September 11, 2015, www.bbc.com/news/technology-34066941.

Jobs that required social skills grew 24 percent between 1980 and 2012. Jobs built on repetitive tasks (garbage collecting, some analytical work) declined. The findings help explain a mystery that has been puzzling economists: the slowdown in the growth even of high-skill jobs. The jobs hardest hit seem to be jobs that don't require social skills, throughout the wage spectrum."[18]

So, what are the implications of the rise of the machines on long-range career planning? It's pretty simple: make sure that you end up with human skills that are differentiated and complementary to what machines can do. If all you are doing is routine calculating, reporting, or execution, you should worry. If you are pursuing a job with high repeatability and low social inputs, you should *really* worry. And you should act. If you don't do something about it, at some point in the future you will be surpassed, replaced, or marginalized by a machine.

After my visit to IBM's TJ Watson Research Center, I drew up a chart to summarize my observations about what humans do well and what machines do well.

In simple terms, we could divide all activities in the world into things that are "repeatable" and those that are "creative." By repeatable, I mean things like mass production, programmatic calculations, and other mechanical tasks. In this domain, the machines dominate. They are better, more accurate, faster, more reliable, and more efficient. In the creative domain, humans still dominate. We are good at things like inventing new ideas, dealing with ambiguity,

---

18 See Claire Cain Miller, "Why What You Learned in Preschool Is Crucial at Work," *New York Times*, October 18, 2015.

HUMAN & MACHINE

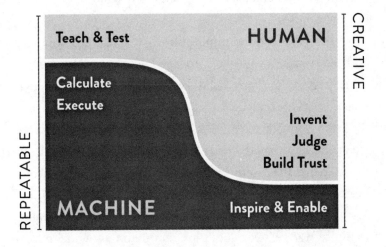

and building human trust. But what is interesting is how humans and machines need to interact. Even in repeatable tasks, there is a critical role for human skills—in teaching the machine, inspecting the output to make sure it is right, and in testing new hypotheses. And in the creative world, there is a growing opportunity to use a machine to assist the creative process. Composers use software to write down the notes and transpose keys—so that the artist can focus on the invention part rather than the laborious mechanics. The modern choreographer can use YouTube searches to find video examples of the greatest Balinese dances in history in order to inspire a new ballet. The oncologist can deploy IBM Watson to help digest millions of data points to help her narrow down the possible treatment options in a complex cancer diagnosis. I encourage people to look up and down the curve and find their home. The greatest danger lurks at the extremes. There are many great roles along the way. Build a skill set that is abundant in the ability to invent, judge, build human trust, interact socially, teach the machines, and create test hypotheses.

This has profound implications for career development and education. We need to spend a disproportionate percentage of our time building the differentiated skills that machines can't match. Says David Autor, an economist at MIT: "If it's just a technical skill, there's a reasonable chance it can be automated. And if it's just being empathetic or flexible, there's an infinite supply of people, so a job won't be well paid. It's the interaction of both that is virtuous." Michael Horn, cofounder of the Clayton Christensen Institute, agrees: "Machines are automating a whole bunch of these things, so having softer skills, knowing the human touch, and how to complement technology is critical. And our education system is not set up for that. To prepare students for the change in the way we work, the skills that schools teach may need to change. Social skills are rarely emphasized in traditional education." David Deming, author and Associate Professor of Education and Economics at Harvard University observes that the only part of our education system that matches the work needs of the future might be preschools. We start out learning about sharing, negotiating, cooperating, and creating. But then as students progress through the system, we replace it with teaching of harder skills. "Work, meanwhile, has become more like preschool." Writes Cain Miller, "Someday, nearly all work could be automated, leaving humans to revel in never-ending leisure time. But in the meantime, this research argues, students should be prepared for the actual world of work.

Maybe high schools and colleges should evaluate students the way preschools do—whether they play well with others."

One company that is on a mission to teach a next generation to fend for themselves in a world of machines is the innovative creative computing company Kano. Cofounders Yonatan Raz-Fridman, Alex Klein, and Saul Klein wondered if they could make a computer that kids of all ages wouldn't just use, but could actually build themselves. Saul's six-year-old son Micah made an inspiring comment: "I'd like to build my own computer, but it needs to be as simple and fun as Lego so no one has to teach me."

So Kano created a computer that kids six and up could assemble, customize, and program by themselves. As Yonatan says: "Kids as young as six or eight can build things of real value. We need a world full of people who can create. We hope to empower a world of mini-entrepreneurs. Unleash the tools and use them to create." Kano is helping to establish a generation of creator-entrepreneurs who build machines so that they won't end up being replaced by them.

There is no question that we will see new styles of work and play in the years ahead. Maybe if we want to see a glimpse of the future of work and education, we should pay special attention to Matthew Brimer. Matthew is the cofounder of an innovative and disruptive educational institution called General Assembly. And he is also the reason I went to a dance party last summer—in the morning.

On a Tuesday in August, 2015, I was up at 4:57 a.m., and just before 6:00 a.m. boarded a huge boat in New York

Harbor. Within a few minutes, the throbbing electronic dance music had whipped the crowd of some 1,200 millennial early-risers into a frenzy. They periodically refueled with snacks of green juice and cricket powder energy bars. Matthew, the host, crowd-surfed to celebrate his twenty-ninth birthday, while the dance floor was invaded by a horn band, and then by dancing vegetables. Needless to say, as a lifelong night owl and dedicated carnivore, I found that the event disrupted my natural biorhythms. And that's the whole point. The event is called Daybreaker, cofounded by Matthew Brimer, social experimenter and entrepreneur. Here is his story.

Profile: Carpe Diem

MATTHEW O. BRIMER
Age 29

Role	Cofounder of General Assembly and Daybreaker
Sweet Spot	Community, education and transformation

There aren't many people who would look at a campus renovation project and see a business opportunity, but Matthew Brimer has always been able to spot the potential that others might miss.

"In our freshman year, my roommates and I discovered that Yale was renovating old buildings and selling antique furniture at huge discounts. So we went down to the warehouse to see what they were getting rid of. We bought an old card catalog for fifty dollars that we later sold for a thousand," Matthew explained. And so a business was born. The next time Matthew and his roommates visited the Yale warehouses they came with their own moving trucks and cleared out most of the inventory. "We rented our own warehouse to store everything, created an e-commerce site and eBay store, and started selling off pieces of inventory. We marketed it as an opportunity to own an invaluable piece of history from a world-class educational institution. We even created certificates of authenticity that we shipped with each piece." Eventually, Yale's renovation project came to a close, and their inventory dried up, bringing the business to a natural conclusion, but for Matthew it was a fascinating experience about learning the ins and outs of running a small business and a powerful lesson in seizing opportunity.

Over the course of his sociology undergraduate studies at Yale, Matthew started another business called GoCrossCampus, a social gaming platform he hoped to pursue full time after graduation. Unfortunately, the app wasn't doing as well as he'd hoped, and Matthew began to take on freelance web design jobs in New York City, learning the ins and outs of the business as he went. He noticed how technology was changing the way people were working, especially those who were around his age. "Work isn't a different thing from life. It's not just about working to make money, but the work you're doing being something that's enjoyable and meaningful in its own right," he explained. "That shifted the traditional work dynamic in a big way." There was a demand for skill sets and opportunities that would help people live and work to take advantage of these digital advancements.

Once again, Matthew spotted an opportunity. "Being

at the center of the tech scene in New York allowed us to be on the pulse of what was being talked about, and what was needed. We started talking to employers to really understand their demands and what they were looking for." He cofounded General Assembly, a hub for the New York start-up ecosystem, with three of his friends. General Assembly began by offering coworking space to up and coming entrepreneurs, but soon evolved to an educational model. As Matthew describes it, they are now "focused on providing transformative education in tech, design, and business to empower a global community so that they can pursue the work they love." General Assembly offers daytime, nighttime, and online courses, ranging from an hour and a half short-form classes to weekend workshops to intensive three-month-long programs for people changing careers.

Matthew's entrepreneurial nature stems in large part from his childhood in St. Louis where his parents, both small business owners, encouraged creativity and finding your own path. "We were a 'maker' household before it really became a term," Matthew recalled. "We had a wood shop in our basement and we were always making things and designing stuff as kids. My parents never had specific career paths in mind for me, but they fostered an entrepreneurial spirit for sure."

Today, General Assembly has become a global enterprise with fourteen campuses across four continents including locations in Sydney, Hong Kong, Singapore, and London. Since its inception in 2011, Matt and his cofounders have raised close to $100 million in funding to continue to expand their operations.

The greatest rewards for Matthew have come from

hearing how students have applied the skills they've learned at General Assembly to improve their own lives. He recounted the story of a wounded veteran who came from Iraq and was looking a fresh start. The man was able to use General Assembly's Opportunity Fund, a philanthropic fellowship program that provides financial aid, and mentorship to underrepresented groups, to complete a web development program, enabling him to get hired as a software engineer.

In his spare time, Matthew is an enthusiastic participant in Burning Man, an annual festival held in Black Rock Desert in Nevada. Despite the inhospitable environment, 75,000 devotees descend and create a temporary city filled with art, dance, and music. He noticed that many aspects of festival culture, in particular the use of drugs, alcohol, and the hard partying, was at odds with the health-conscious values of many of his friends. Spotting another opportunity, he cofounded his latest venture, Daybreaker, a mix between a social experiment, an art project, and a really great party.

Daybreaker takes inspiration from festivals like Burning Man and creates community events around music, tribalism, connection, dance, and wellbeing—values that Matthew feels are increasingly important to his generation. The events focus on the artistic aspects of rave experiences (think DJs and dancing) but instead of consuming alcohol, participants drink green smoothies and juices and cold-brew coffees. Event organizers also feature spoken word poets, yoga instructors, and meditation sessions—oh, and like the name implies, the events take place really early in the morning. It's for people who want to start their workday with a boost of energy and endorphins earned from hitting the dance floor. It was a success: the first-ever event sold 150 tickets for the

6:00 a.m. starting time and has been growing in popularity ever since. Much like General Assembly, Matthew has once again designed a unique space for experiencing community. Daybreaker events have already happened in ten cities in four countries, with plans for more hot cities like Dubai and Berlin well underway. In early 2016, Brimer expanded the Daybreaker concept with a new idea called Dusk. The first Dusk was held at a synagogue in New York City and attracted over eight hundred young people of all religions to dance and celebrate in the early evening.

For Brimer, success is helping those around him succeed. "Everyone is coming in from different backgrounds and experiences. Everyone is unique," he said. "The whole goal here has been to empower people to pursue the goals they want, and the ambitions and pursuits they are passionate about."

As we think about a future led by Watsons and Matthew Brimer, we need to prepare ourselves to find satisfying and vibrant work. Developing our emotional, creative, collaborative, and trust-building selves looks like a really smart career bet for the future.

Where and How Will I Find Work in the Future?

As we look ahead to a new era of education and work, how will each of us fit in? Looking ten, twenty, and thirty years into the future, where will we find work and how will we find it? One model that is certain to get some serious airplay is "data-driven career matchmaking." We have already seen the massive expansion of digital job posting sites like Indeed, Monster.com, Glassdoor, CareerBuilder, and others. LinkedIn has become a global talent powerhouse, with over 400 million members in two hundred countries. Online "matching" for romantic relationships is already pervasive in our society. Statistics Brain reports that over fifty million Americans have tried online dating, and Match.com has well over twenty million members.[19]

If digital technology and data can already post hundreds of millions of jobs and connect millions of us romantically, where can the matchmaking of jobseekers and talent-hungry companies go in the future? LinkedIn CEO Jeff Weiner is on a mission to create a global "economic graph" within a decade. He aims to include all the job listings in the world, all the skills required to get those jobs, all the educational institutions who teach those skills, all the professionals who could fill them, and all the companies and non-profit organizations at which they work. LinkedIn is already providing deep filtering of search criteria (e.g. "Find engineers with Hadoop experience in Brazil") and highlighting hotspots in demand and supply for specific skill sets. The ultimate goal is to make the world economy and job market more efficient through increased transparency. In this new world, job-seekers would be better able to "shop" for employers and for the educational institutions who can help them build the most personally relevant and in-demand skills. As part of this mission, LinkedIn has recently invested in Lynda.com, which offers an extensive curriculum of video courses. LinkedIn wants to become a tool that predicts what

---

19 Statisticsbrain.com Online Dating—data from November 2015.

promotions or jobs users will want next and to automatically suggest Lynda courses to help workers get there.

With data-driven matchmaking, educational institutions would be better equipped to find students and to offer curriculums attuned to employer needs. Employers would have access to much broader and deeper talent pools, especially for niche skills in high-demand areas. Before long, we will be seeing "predictive career planning" where the huge skill marketplaces like LinkedIn can begin to predict where the supply and demand of skills will go—by country and industry, right down to the individual. In this future world, career-minded individuals would need an even firmer hand on their career destiny—listening to their hearts, to the job opportunity marketplace, and becoming savvy shoppers for skills and work.

Not everyone believes that the world is ready for the data-driven vision of the job marketplace. In June 2015, Dan Goleman—the author of *Emotional Intelligence* we met back in chapter 3—wrote an open letter to Jeff Weiner, CEO of LinkedIn. Here is an extract from that original letter:

> Dear Jeff:
>
> There's no doubt that LinkedIn has become the world's best place to connect professionally and build your network. I see a way it could be even better. It comes down to the fact that character counts, not just credentials and job experience.
>
> LinkedIn profiles understandably emphasize professional accomplishments. But your expertise, experience and accomplishments are just one dimension of who you are. Technically, these

indicate "threshold" competencies—the abilities someone needs for a given position. What they don't indicate is what kind of person you are. And that can make all the difference. In the HR world these are "distinguishing" abilities, the ones that set star performers apart from mediocre. One aspect of distinguishing abilities is your emotional intelligence—how you handle yourself and your relationships. Are you self-aware? Do you stay calm and clear during a crisis? Can you stay focused on your long-term goals? Do you tune in to other people? Listen? Communicate effectively? Collaborate well? But who you are goes beyond such emotional intelligence competencies to include your character. Do you have integrity? Are you compassionate? Character counts. As Fred Kiel found, managers high in character traits like integrity and compassion got business results *five times greater* than those with fewer positive character traits.

Goleman goes on to suggest that activities related to character-building and emotional intelligence (such as volunteer work, causes you care about, corporate responsibility, etc.) should get much more prominence in how LinkedIn captures our skills profiles. I agree with Daniel Goleman's assertion that skills inventories must include factors like character and emotional intelligence if they are to enable successful matches. Ultimately, as in the man versus machine debate, the answer for employee-employer matchmaking will likely be a hybrid between very data-driven and very human models. Talent databases will do more and more to identify, source, and prescreen skill sets, and wise humans will be needed to make the final enlightened decisions on what talent will truly inspire top performance.

How Will I Spend My Time?

As Carl Sandburg tells us in chapter 6, "Time is the only coin of our lives." How on earth are we going to spend it in the future?

The first point to make is that we are certainly going to have a lot more total coins of time to spend, and that will have big implications on how we view work. As Lynda Gratton, London Business School professor and cofounder of the Future of Work initiative says: "What happens to work when people live for a hundred years? This question may seem incredibly future-focused, however, it's happening faster than you think. Indeed, 50 percent of babies born today in the UK will live to 103 and this increases to 107 for those born in Japan. And it's not just newborns that are likely to be centurions. If you are 60 and have not suffered any serious health concerns, you are well positioned to reach the big 100…. Not only are older members of society finding themselves needing or wanting to work past traditional retirement ages, but people of all age groups are having to adjust their progression plans and working styles to ensure they have the right skills and requisite energy levels for long careers."[20]

---

20 See Lynda Gratton's website, The Future of Work (www.lyndagrattonfutureofwork.typepad.com), for additional statistics and trends on work.

There is no doubt that we are going to see "long-tail careers" that extend well into our late sixties, seventies, and even eighties. The nature and objective of the work will likely change. Traditionally careers have focused primarily on the corporate sector, and on "making a good living." In the future, I see a dramatic expansion of entrepreneurial and freelance options, and a more diverse set of goals for work. Creating a business where you can sell goods and services online is already becoming a pervasive source of income and engagement for many people in late-stage careers, and this will accelerate. Freelance work is the hottest growth sector in the labor economy. There are already fifty-four million freelancers in America across all age groups. More than half do freelance work by choice, not by necessity, and advances in technology and social networking are making it easier to find and perform freelance assignments.[21] Freelance work can be a great pillar in a long-tail career of the future. It offers "mastery for hire" in exchange for income. Putting our skills up for sale forces us to stay fresh. The hours are more flexible and work can often be done remotely. Freelance assignments can provide interesting work and interaction at a time when you have a lot more time on your hands. We should all think hard about our long-tail careers and how we will find purpose, flexibility, refreshment, and income in the years past typical retirement.

---

21 Edelman & Berland October 2015 Survey on the Freelance Economy.

Will I Outlast My Money?

The critical need for income in retirement is a big and scary coming attraction for aging populations everywhere. The statistics are startling: the average American has a net worth of just over $300,000 at age sixty-five.[22] If they stop work completely and invest it all, this creates an estimated annual income of less than $20,000 per year. Even if the retirement nest egg increases to $1 million the resulting annual income is still only about $50,000.[23] To make matters worse, we can no longer rely on other traditional sources of retirement income to fill the gap. Company pensions and government assistance no longer provide as much bridging and support as they did in the past. When interest rates were high, we could put our assets into income-producing bonds and happily live off the interest. But today, interest rates are at historic lows and are not expected to rebound any time soon. So unless you are counting on inherited wealth, windfall investment gains, or winning lottery tickets, you will find yourself like the vast majority of Americans: hungry for sources of income past the age of sixty-five. For many, the answer will be work.

How Will Work Make Me Happy?

If we are destined to be working harder, working longer, foraging for income, and even competing with the machines,

---

22 Median net worth = $309,000. SCF 2013.

23 BlackRock Cost of Retirement Index calculation performed February 28, 2016. Savings at age sixty-five of $309,000 results in estimated annual retirement income of $15,000. Savings of $1 million results in estimated annual income of $48,544.

is there any room left for happiness in the future of work? In my view, the answer is absolutely yes. It starts with what makes us happy. There are many theories, and I have a favorite: it is by Sonja Lyubomirsky, professor at University of California and author of *The How of Happiness*.[24] Dr. Lyubomirsky has dedicated her career as a research scientist to the study of happiness. I like her approach because it encourages us to think about those things we can change. The central premise of *The How of Happiness* is that three main factors explain our levels of happiness: 50 percent of a given human's happiness level is genetically determined, 10 percent is affected by life circumstances, and a remaining 40 percent of happiness is subject to voluntary, intentional activities.

1. Our genetic set point. Lyubomirsky writes: "The set point for happiness is similar to the set point for weight. Some people are blessed with skinny dispositions: even when they're not trying, they easily maintain their weight. By contrast, others have to work extraordinarily hard to keep their weight at a desirable level, and the moment they slack off even a bit, the pounds creep back on."

So those of us with low happiness set points will have to work harder to achieve and maintain happiness, while those of us with high set points will find it easier to be happy under similar conditions.

2. Life circumstances. Our life circumstances—including income—may matter less than we think. Once we achieve a threshold level of material wealth and comfort, our life

---

24 See also Lyubomirsky's Person-Activity Fit Diagnostic, a useful tool to help you choose which of the twelve strategies might work best for you.

circumstances do not seem to explain much about our happiness levels. In fact, some research says that very wealthy people are more anxious than average. Also, there is a body of evidence that increases in our life circumstances may not have lasting effect on happiness levels. Through a process called "hedonistic adaptation," we seem to begin taking things for granted and do not feel the same lift as when we first acquired the new status.

3. Intentional activities. The remaining 40 percent of our happiness is determined by our behavior—the voluntary and intentional acts we take. This is the core of Lyubomirsky's thesis: we can't alter our genetic set points, and changes in life circumstances don't have a lasting impact on our happiness, but we can increase and sustain our happiness through intentional activities. Notes Lyubomirsky: "The secret, of course, lies in the 40 percent. If we observe genuinely happy people, we shall find that they do not just sit around being contented. They make things happen. They pursue new understandings, seek new achievements, and control their thoughts and feelings. In sum, our intentional effortful activities have a powerful effect on how happy we are, over and above the effect of our set points and the circumstances in which we find ourselves. If an unhappy person wants to experience interest, enthusiasm, contentment, peace, and joy, he or she can make it happen by learning the habits of a happy person."

The How of Happiness outlines a dozen "evidence-based happiness-increasing strategies whose practice is supported by scientific research." These include:

- Expressing Gratitude
- Cultivating Optimism
- Avoiding Overthinking and Social Comparison
- Practicing Acts of Kindness
- Nurturing Social Relationships
- Developing Strategies for Coping
- Learning to Forgive
- Increasing Flow Experiences
- Savoring Life's Joys
- Committing to Your Goals
- Practicing Religion and Spirituality
- Taking Care of Your Body

Let me take on three of these, and apply them to work and careers.

1. Increasing flow experiences. The concept of "flow" was initially developed by Mihaly Csíkszentmihályi, currently Distinguished Professor of Psychology at Claremont Graduate University. In *Flow: The Psychology of Optimal Experience*, the author describes flow as "a sense that one's skills are adequate to cope with the challenges at hand. Concentration is so intense that there is no attention left over to think about anything irrelevant, or to worry about problems. Self-consciousness disappears, and the sense of time appears distorted." A person "in flow" has been described as "proceeding in a seamless, spontaneous, adept way, creating a sense of fluidity in one's action."

The experts say that flow is something beneficial that we should actively seek. "In our studies, we found that every flow activity…had this in common: It provided a sense of discovery, a creative feeling of transporting the person into a new reality. It pushed the person to higher levels of performance, and led to previously undreamed-of states of consciousness. Lyubomirsky agrees: "To maintain flow, we continually have to test ourselves in ever more challenging activities.... We have to stretch our skills or find novel opportunities to use them. This is wonderful, because it means that we are constantly striving, growing, learning, and becoming more competent, expert, and complex."[25]

I think we all occasionally experience the precious feeling of flow. For me, flow might occur when we present a striking new creative idea to a client. Or when we win a new business, pitted against the world's best competition. I might experience flow speaking on stage about a topic I am deeply passionate about. I occasionally feel the magic of flow when playing with my rock band. Sometimes we are so in sync that the band seems to rise up like a sailboat lifting out of the water on a windy day. When do you feel the flow? What gives you the most enjoyment? What absorbs you? What activities leave you with the feeling that the time has passed incredibly fast? Flow is good. In your career, become a flow-seeking missile.

2. Committing to your goals. The scientists assert that having a clear plan actually makes you happier. This has big implications for how you approach career planning. Stop worrying and take action. Seize control of those things you can influence. Devote at least one full day each year to career reflection and strategy. Take inventory. Test

---

25   See also Ed Batista, "Sonja Lyubomirsky and The How of Happiness," edbatista. com, February 8, 2009, www.edbatista.com/2009/02/happiness.html.

out some hypotheses. Set ambitions. Constantly build and refresh your fuel. Monitor your progress. Remain in perpetual discovery mode and listen for opportunity. Prepare yourself for a thrilling and uncertain future. And enjoy the long ride.

3. Express gratitude. My final thought for this book is on expressing gratitude. According to research, the act of saying thank you empirically makes us feel better. A few years ago, my father died at age eighty-seven after a long, eclectic, and successful life.[26] During my father's last weeks, his favorite word was "grateful." He was grateful that you showed up, grateful for a cup of tea or glass of water, grateful that you played his favorite old song, and grateful that you moved a pillow over three inches. He was very happy in his gratitude.

In our work lives, we all need to be grateful—as employees, grateful to those who give us opportunities, raises, promotions, assignments, and chances to grow. We should be grateful to those who share their gifts of wisdom with us. As employers, we must also be grateful to the people who work with and for us, for dedicating their talents, energies, passions and skills to our cause.

In closing, I am eternally grateful for every job I have ever had.

---

26 I wrote up a carefully crafted obituary that listed my father's various law degrees, volunteer roles, and professional accomplishments. It was far outshone by a local French-language newspaper whose headline referred to him as "l'avocat pour tout"—the champion for all.

Paid Jobs I've Done in My Life and What I Learned

Gardener: First job	The value of a dollar
Snow removal contractor	Canadian winters last forever
Window cleaner	Pricing by job, not by hour
House painter	The power of word-of-mouth referrals
Baby sitter	Responsibility
Dog sitter	Coping with allergies
Golf caddie	Customer service, stamina
Baseball umpire	Judgment, dealing with angry adults
Carpet salesman	Bundling products together
Door-to-door salesman	Overcoming fear of rejection
Dishwasher	Humility
Bartender	Customer empathy
Insurance accountant	Accounting methods
Market researcher	Making data into insights
Whiskey barrel salesman	Advertising actually works
Marketing consultant	How to make clear recommendations
Exam invigilator	There's good money in compliance
College lecturer	Statistics and HR
President of a small company	How to budget and pay off bank loans
Brand manager	A brand is more than a product
Advertising executive	Stay very close to customers
Author	The words don't just write themselves
Musician for a garage band	There's no money in rhythm guitar and blues harmonica

Acknowledgments

There are an immense number of people who made this book possible.

First, I thank my family—my wife Chris, my daughters Claire and Alison, my mother Cathy Fetherstonhaugh in Montreal, my brother Rob, and my sister Catherine. They have showered me with love, support, and good ideas throughout my life and throughout this project. Chris went far beyond the call of duty to read and review every word of every draft manuscript, and made the book better every single time. I am sorry my father could not be with us to see this book come to life, but I hope he is up there somewhere nodding approvingly and discussing the book with complete strangers.

I never really planned to write a book, but was inspired and cajoled by several people early in the process. The author Rahaf Harfoush urged me to write up my advice and share it enthusiastically with others. She became a critical researcher, interviewer, profile writer, and advisor to me throughout the process.

Jeremy Katz helped me land my first magazine article for *Fast Company* that formed the initial premise of this book. Lorraine Shanley encouraged me to write, and introduced me to the legendary literary agent Jim Levine.

Thank you to the entire Diversion Books team— publisher Jaime Levine, editor Randall Klein, Chris Mahon on marketing, Sarah Masterson Hally on design, and our initial contact Mary Cummings.

I am immensely grateful to the Ogilvy team including Mish Fletcher, Joseph Nostro, Stefan Mreczko, Ken McVeagh, and to Elli Hanson for her superb work on book design. Thank you to the Ogilvy Young Professional Network team including Shelin Mei, Casey Lewis, Charlotte Spatcher, Alessia Morales, and especially to the dynamo, Daniel Jeydel, who worked tirelessly on research, interviewing, and digital marketing. Thanks also to my fellow execs John Seifert, Scott Murphy, Miles Young, Gunther Schumacher, Lou Aversano, Carla Hendra, and Dimitri Maex for their ongoing support.

This book would not be possible without the insights and wisdom of the many people we interviewed, consulted and profiled in *The Long View*:

Mohammed Ashour, Yves Baudechon, Milena Berry, Paul Berry, Matt Blumberg, Matt Breitfelder, Matthew Brimer, Jim Bunn, Susan Cain, Bill Carr, Irena Choi Stern, Dorie Clark, Justin Cruanes, Jessica Di Pietro, William Forrester, Dr. Jules Goddard, Thomas Graf, Adam M. Grant, Chris Graves, Laura Harrison, Todd Herman, Auren

Hoffman, Allan Houston, Rob Jessup-Ramsay, Brian Jolson, Janet Kestin, Saken Kulkarni, Steve Landsberg, Shelly Lazarus, Mark Linaugh, Andrea Longueira, Susan Machtiger, John Mannhart, Nilofer Merchant, Felim McGrath, Dr. Karl Moore, Rachel S. Moore, Lara O'Shea, Tim Penner, Daniel Pink, Susan Piper, Gordon Polatnick, Tom Pritchard, Tom Rath, Yonatan Raz-Fridman, Chuck Reese, Linda Robinson, Anthony Rodriguez, Kathleen Ryan, Stephen Sacca, Alvaro Saralegui, Jann Martin Schwarz, Peter Sims, Benjamin Snyers, Sir Martin Sorrell, Rory Sutherland, Don Tapscott, Linda Turner, Nancy Vonk, Barbara Waldorf, Alex White, David Wilkin, Tracy Wolstencroft, John Wood

I apologize to those who I have accidentally missed from this list. I am grateful to you all!

Finally, I would like to acknowledge three immense influences in my own career. Tro Piliguian was my boss and mentor at Ogilvy Canada and later in New York. He gave me the confidence to tackle the global stage, and generously passed along the wisdom of a lifetime, almost always over a delicious Italian meal and a glass of wine. The legendary Steve Hayden was my creative partner during the formative stages of my career, and taught me the unstoppable power of big ideas and sparkling talent. And I have had the immense privilege of working with and for the extraordinary Shelly Lazarus for over twenty years. Shelly has always been an inspirational example of what a leader can be—strong, smart, clear, fair, warm, and thoroughly human.

Key References
& Suggested Reading

Bradberry, Travis and Greaves, Jean. *Emotional Intelligence 2.0*. TalentSmart, 2009.

Cain, Susan. *Quiet*. Broadway Books, 2012.

Casnocha, Ben and Hoffman, Reid. *The Start-Up of You*. Crown Business, 2012.

Clark, Dorie. *Stand Out: How to Find Your Breakthrough Idea and Build a Following Around It*. Portfolio, 2015.

Gladwell, Malcolm. *Outliers*. Little, Brown & Company, 2008.

Goleman, Daniel. *Working With Emotional Intelligence*. Bantam, 2011.

Grant, Adam M. *Give and Take*. Penguin Books, 2013.

Grant, Adam M. *Originals: How Non-Conformists Move the World*. Viking, 2016.

Gratton, Lynda. *The Shift: The Future of Work is Already Here*. HarperCollins Business, 2011.

Gratton, Lynda and Scott, Andrew. *The 100-Year Life: Living and Working in an Age of Longevity.* Featherstone Education, 2016.

Kahneman, Daniel. *Thinking Fast and Slow.* Farrar, Straus and Giroux, 2013.

Kestin, Janet and Vonk, Nancy. *Darling You Can't Do Both (And Other Noise You Should Ignore on Your Way Up).* Harper, 2014.

Lyubomirsky, Sonja. *The How of Happiness.* Penguin Books, 2008.

Moore, Rachel S. *The Artist's Compass.* Touchstone, 2016.

Rath, Tom. *StrengthsFinder 2.0.* Gallup Press, 2007.

Rath, Tom. *Are You Fully Charged?: The 3 Keys to Energizing Your Work and Life.* Silicon Guild, 2015.

Sims, Peter. *Small Bets: How Breakthrough Ideas Emerge from Small Discoveries.* Simon & Schuster, 2013.

Sutherland, Rory. *The Wiki Man.* It's Nice That, Ogilvy Digital Labs, 2011.

Taleb, Nassim Nicholas. *Antifragile: This That Gain from Disorder.* Random House Trade Paperbacks, 2014.

Tapscott, Don and Alex. *Blockchain Revolution.* Portfolio, 2014.

Yeh, Chris and Hoffman, Reid. *The Alliance: Managing Talent in the Networked Age.* Harvard Business Review Press, 2014.

Brian Fetherstonhaugh
Chairman & CEO
OgilvyOne Worldwide

Brian brings a fresh and authoritative view to both sides of the career equation.

For the past 10 years he's been the global CEO of a leading 5,000+ person digital marketing company, working with top brands such as IBM, American Express, Coca-Cola, IKEA, Unilever, and Nestlé. In this capacity he's helped to start and develop the careers of thousands of individuals and observed the trajectories of people at all career stages.

Over the past two decades Brian has also become a respected career mentor and thought leader. He has lectured on career strategy at institutions including Yale, Harvard, MIT Sloan School, Columbia, and McGill.

He is also the executive sponsor for Ogilvy's Young Professional Network and is an advisor to several start-ups. Brian has been a board member of Goodwill Industries for over 20 years and is a passionate supporter of its mission to help people gain independence through the power of work.

Brian was born and raised in Montréal, Canada, and now resides in New York with his wife, Chris. He plays hockey on Sunday nights, and plays guitar and harmonica in a rock band, aptly named Plan B.